REAL MEXICAN FOOD
FOR PEOPLE
WITH DIABETES

REAL MEXICAN FOOD FOR PEOPLE WITH DIABETES

DORIS CROSS

PRIMA HEALTH
A DIVISION OF PRIMA PUBLISHING

Warning—disclaimer

This book is not intended to provide medical advice and is sold with the understanding that the publisher and the author are not liable for the misconception or misuse of information provided. The author and Prima Publishing shall have neither liability nor responsibility to any person or entity with respect to any loss, damage, or injury caused or alleged to be caused directly or indirectly by the information contained in this book or the use of any products mentioned. Readers should not use any of the products discussed in this book without the advice of a medical professional.

Nutritional Analyses

A per serving nutritional breakdown is provided for each recipe. If a range is given for an ingredient amount, the breakdown is based on the smaller number. If a range is given for servings, the breakdown is based on the larger number. If a choice of ingredients is given in an ingredient listing, the breakdown is calculated using the first choice. Nutritional content may vary depending on the specific brands or types of ingredients used. "Optional" ingredients or those for which no specific amount is stated are not included in the breakdown.

On the cover: *Spicy Steak Soup (page 21), Jalapeño Corn Bread with Cheese (page 242), and Southwest Chicken Wraps (page 186).*

PRIMA HEALTH and colophon are trademarks of Prima Communications, Inc.

Interior illustrations by Mary Rich

Library of Congress Cataloging-in-Publication Data

Cross, Doris.
  Real Mexican food for people with diabetes / Doris Cross.
    p.   cm.
  Includes index.
  ISBN 0-7615-1431-7
  1. Diabetes—Diet therapy—Recipes.   2. Cookery, Mexican.   I. Title.
RC662.C764   1998
641.5′6314—dc21   98-28209
                                                                CIP

98 99 00 01 DD 10 9 8 7 6 5 4 3 2 1

Printed in the United States of America

HOW TO ORDER

Single copies may be ordered from Prima Publishing, P.O. Box 1260BK, Rocklin, CA 95677; telephone (916) 632-4400. Quantity discounts are also available. On your letterhead, include information concerning the intended use of the books and the number of books you wish to purchase.

Visit us online at www.primahealth.com

TO TONY, TRACI, ROWDY,
AND THAT "NEW LITTLE BABY MARYLIN" -
AND
MIKE, GABRIEL, AND RALSTON

Contents

ACKNOWLEDGMENTS

It is hard for me to find the right words to thank everyone, because there are just so many people to whom I am indebted. I would first like to say thank you to Prima Publishing and to my editor Jamie Miller. I feel so lucky to have the sweetest and the best editor as well as the greatest publisher.

The Merrill family ranks at the top of my list of those to whom I am eternally grateful. I would never have owned a computer, much less been able to type recipes on it, if it were not for Hugh. Hugh keeps my computer going and, consequently, keeps *me* going. Hugh's wife, Kathy, and his daughter, Rhonda, have helped me tremendously with typing and organizing. Thanks guys, and we promise to have you over for frosting again very soon.

To all of the very special people in my family whom I love, as well as all the friends I have mentioned before, I would like to say thank you. These people have always believed in me and in whatever I wanted to do.

Alice Williams is one who deserves a big medal for putting up with all my ups and downs, as do Rick, Rodette, and Staci Green. Rick, because he is simply the best; Staci, because she is my right hand and the person I can always depend on; and Rodette, for literally carrying the office business while I struggled to quit smoking. It's been tough, but I'm proud to say, I've made it five months as a nonsmoker.

This fact brings me to my doctors and their office personnel. Dr. Kathleen Harder is the best in the whole world. She just seems to know when it's time to be stern with me and when it's time to be kind and understanding. Thank you Dr. Rob Harder for originally diagnosing my diabetes and for sending me to the right people for the best care. Jeannie Drew is a special gal who is sweet, kind, and understanding. Connie Ralston and Diana Spiva are also wonderful and round out the office crew. Thank you gals, I appreciate you all for caring about me personally.

Professionally, I don't know where I would be without Erma, Elmo, and all my special friends back east who work so tirelessly to see that my books are displayed in a favorable light. Likewise, I would be lost without Adran Wagner, my CPA. If you live in Stillwater, Oklahoma, go to her. If you don't live here, weep!

Of course, Sharon Brown, Abby Stokes, and Hannah Stokes are three of the most special people in my life and are my very best friends whom I cherish.

A very special thank you to my dear friends: Maurice Gershon, Michael Morgan, Janelle Walker, Brandon Barnes, Gina Morris, and Lisa Coburn.

A final thanks to Kevin Miller and Stacy Croft. Kevin is one of the nicest young men who has ever worked for me. Someday he is going to be a famous musician! Stacy is a wonderful proofreader and recipe tester. She's neat, and I don't know what I would have done without her. She saved my life with this book.

It is just so nice to work with this many great people. I feel I am truly blessed to be surrounded by such wonderful people!

INTRODUCTION

Welcome to cooking and eating Mexican food for diabetics at its very best. After years of owning my own weight-loss clinic, I have found that Mexican and Southwestern foods are the foods people crave the most when they are restricting what they eat.

If you have purchased any of my other cookbooks, then you already know that not only have I lost 100 pounds but I have also managed to keep the weight off for about ten years. Until five months ago, I felt very much in control of my eating. Then, I encountered my worst struggle to date with my weight loss. I quit smoking! I had never been a nervous eater, but I am now and I've gained weight. Yet, I know that as soon as I have made it through a few more months as a nonsmoker, I will be successful and I will lose the weight I have gained. This is one of the most important concepts that I try to teach people who want to lose weight. Never, never give up on yourself! If you have a bad day, get up, brush yourself off, and go at it again. Eat for your health, but at the same time, do not look at the changes in your food as a diet.

Being on a very strict diet makes us all crazy. So, be kind to yourself in every way possible and try not to put yourself in a position where you are focusing on food.

All of my recipes are lowfat and low-calorie versions of the foods you love to eat. I would classify most of my recipes as medium hot, which allows you to add more hot pepper if you desire.

At the request of people attending my seminars, I have included something new in this cookbook. I have included more recipes for just two or three people. While I am happy to fulfill this request, I have to admit that a problem has been created. The problem is what to do with the ingredients remaining in the cans, cartons, and so on that you didn't use in the recipe. Thus, you have recipes for only two or three people but now you are faced with the dilemma of what to do with the leftover ingredients! For now, I will leave this problem for you to ponder.

I absolutely love putting things together that make people happy. Especially if it is something that allows people to eat foods they thought they would have to give up. Eating lowfat and sugar-free is not what it used to be. Today, there are many foods and products available that are so fun! I have used all of these new fat-free and lowfat products on the market in an attempt to show people that they can still eat very good food.

This cookbook is full of lots of yummy stuff. I hope you enjoy it.

I would like to now share information about some outstanding products I have come across during my years in the weight-loss business. These products are my absolute favorites, and I hope you will try them!

Cabot Farms 75 percent Reduced Fat Cheddar Cheese: This is a most heavenly white Cheddar cheese with only 2½ grams of fat per ounce. This cheese tastes like full-fat

Cheddar and grates and melts beautifully. For quality and taste, I have not found an equal on the market today. This product is widely available on the East Coast; if you live elsewhere, you may get it by mail-order. I think it is worth the extra effort to order it! To contact Cabot Farms' mail-order department, call (800) 639-3198.

Buttermist cooking spray is a butter-flavored nonstick spray that tastes wonderful! It is my all-time favorite spray—I use it every day, and I'm not sure I could live without it! It has about the same number of calories and grams of fat as other cooking sprays, but the difference is in the taste. Spray it on toast, bagels, English muffins, popcorn, or anything that needs "butter." This product is not water based, so it won't make your popcorn soggy. The flavor is best if bread items are sprayed before toasting.

Buttermist cannot be found in supermarkets. Because it is so good and not available in stores, I decided to make it available by shipping it through mail order so other people could enjoy it, too. The cans are 14-ounce commercial size.

To order Buttermist by Visa or Mastercard, call my office and leave your order on the answering machine: (405) 372-4105. To order by mail, send a check for $19.50, which includes shipping and handling, for two 14-ounce cans to the following address:

Doris' Diet Recipes
P.O. Box 549
Stillwater, OK 74076

(Sorry, we are not allowed to ship to Canada.)

1

SOUPS, SALADS, AND APPETIZERS

ZESTY CREAM CHEESE DIP

SERVES 4

1 tub (8 ounces) fat-free cream cheese
3 tablespoons salsa
1 clove garlic, pressed
1 tablespoon seeded and finely chopped bell pepper
1 tablespoon dry onion flakes
½ small jalapeño pepper, seeds removed and chopped (optional)

In medium bowl, cream fat-free cream cheese with electric mixer. When it is smooth and creamy, add salsa, garlic, bell pepper, onion flakes, and optional jalapeño pepper and mix. Chill before serving. Delicious served with lowfat chips or crackers.

Each serving provides:

56	Calories	0.5 g	Fiber
0.1 g	Fat	330 mg	Sodium
7.9 g	Protein	4 mg	Cholesterol
5.6 g	Carbohydrates		

Diabetic exchanges: Lean meat, ½; starch, ⅓

Steak Soup

Serves 6

⅓ pound fajita-style sliced beef
   Garlic salt
   Black pepper
1 small onion, chopped
2 cans (14½ ounces each) beef broth
1 can (10¾ ounces) Campbell's 98 percent fat-free condensed cream of mushroom soup
1 package (1 ounce) dry ranch dressing mix
2½ cups water
1 large potato, peeled and cut into chunks
½ cup fat-free sour cream

Spray large saucepan with nonstick cooking spray. Brown beef strips over medium heat for 2 to 3 minutes. Season with garlic salt and black pepper to taste. Add onion and brown. Add beef broth, cream of mushroom soup, dressing mix, and water. Simmer over low heat 45 minutes to 1 hour. Add potatoes and simmer 20 to 30 minutes, until potatoes are done. Whisk in sour cream and serve.

Each serving provides:

122	Calories	0.6 g	Fiber
3.9 g	Fat	1383 mg	Sodium
9.4 g	Protein	17 mg	Cholesterol
12.4 g	Carbohydrates		

Diabetic exchanges: Lean meat, 1; starch, ⁴⁄₅

PINEAPPLE-COCONUT SHRIMP SALAD

SERVES 4

1 cup cooked macaroni or other pasta
2 tablespoons sliced green onions
¼ cup drained pineapple tidbits
6 large cooked and peeled shrimp, cut into ½-inch pieces
½ cup fat-free mayonnaise
1 tablespoon orange juice
1 teaspoon fresh lime juice
¼ teaspoon coconut extract flavoring
1 packet Sweet 'n Low
  Salt

Rinse cooked pasta in cold water; drain well. In mixing bowl, stir together pasta, green onions, pineapple, and shrimp. In smaller bowl, mix together mayonnaise, orange juice, lime juice, coconut extract, and Sweet 'n Low. Pour over macaroni-shrimp mixture and stir. Salt to taste. Cover and chill in refrigerator until ready to serve.

To serve, spoon salad onto individual iceberg or leaf lettuce leaves.

Each serving provides:

131	Calories	0.8 g	Fiber
0.7 g	Fat	482 mg	Sodium
11.5 g	Protein	88 mg	Cholesterol
18.9 g	Carbohydrates		

Diabetic exchanges: Lean meat, 1; starch, ½; fruit, ⅔

FIESTA PASTA SALAD

SERVES 4

1 cup cooked macaroni or other pasta
¼ cup chopped red onion
¼ cup seeded and chopped red bell pepper
¼ cup seeded and chopped green bell pepper
1 cup frozen corn, thawed
1 tablespoon chopped canned green chilies
½ teaspoon chili powder
¼ teaspoon ground cumin
¼ cup Italian fat-free dressing
1 tablespoon chopped cilantro (optional)
Salt

Rinse cooked pasta and drain well; transfer to serving bowl. In mixing bowl, stir together onion, bell peppers, corn, chilies, chili powder, cumin, dressing, cilantro if desired, and salt to taste. Add to pasta. Chill in refrigerator until ready to serve.

Each serving provides:

99	Calories	2.2 g	Fiber
1.5 g	Fat	218 mg	Sodium
3.2 g	Protein	0 mg	Cholesterol
20.3 g	Carbohydrates		

Diabetic exchanges: Starch, ½; vegetable, 2; fat, ⅓

Mexican Rice and Bean Salad

SERVES 6

1 cup ranch-style beans, rinsed and drained
2 cups cooked rice, cooled
1 cup frozen corn, thawed
¼ cup chopped green onions (white and green part)
¼ cup jarred picante sauce
⅓ cup Italian fat-free dressing
1 tablespoon fresh lime juice
¼ teaspoon ground cumin
   Salt

In mixing bowl, stir together beans, rice, corn, green onions, picante sauce, dressing, lime juice, cumin, and salt to taste. Serve chilled.

Each serving provides:

151	Calories	3 g	Fiber
1.4 g	Fat	360 mg	Sodium
4.7 g	Protein	0 mg	Cholesterol
31.5 g	Carbohydrates		

Diabetic exchanges: Starch, 1½; vegetable, 1; fat, ½

Taco Salad

½ pound ground turkey breast
2 tablespoons fat-free chicken broth
   Salt and black pepper
⅓ cup chopped onion
½ cup chopped tomato
1 cup chopped lettuce
1 cup grated lowfat Cheddar cheese
¾ cup ranch-style beans, rinsed and drained
¾ cup Catalina fat-free dressing
1 cup crushed reduced-fat tortilla chips (see note)

Spray medium skillet with nonstick cooking spray. Brown ground turkey over medium heat, stirring often for 6 to 9 minutes. Add chicken broth during browning to help keep turkey moist. Season browned turkey with salt and pepper to taste; set aside until cooled to room temperature.

Note: Nutrition information may vary depending on nutrition content in reduced-fat tortilla chips.

In large salad bowl, mix turkey, onion, tomato, lettuce, cheese, beans, dressing, and tortilla chips. Serve immediately.

Each serving provides:

393	Calories	4.3 g	Fiber
11.4 g	Fat	756 mg	Sodium
25 g	Protein	63 mg	Cholesterol
46.7 g	Carbohydrates		

Diabetic exchanges: Lean meat, 2; vegetable, 2; starch, 3

Red Hot Corn Chowder

Serves 2

1 can (14½ ounces) fat-free chicken broth
1 green onion, chopped
1 small clove garlic, pressed
⅓ cup grated carrots
¾ cup water
½ fresh jalapeño pepper, seeded and sliced (see note)
  Salt and black pepper
1 cup frozen corn, thawed
⅓ cup fat-free sour cream

In saucepan, combine chicken broth, green onion, garlic, carrots, water, jalapeño pepper, and salt and pepper to taste. Simmer over low heat until carrots are done, 10 to 15 minutes. Add corn and simmer about 2 minutes. Whisk in sour cream and cook about 2 minutes. Serve.

Each serving provides:

124	Calories	2.9 g	Fiber
0.4 g	Fat	942 mg	Sodium
7.5 g	Protein	0 mg	Cholesterol
25.6 g	Carbohydrates		

Diabetic exchange: Starch, 1½

Note: Adjust jalapeño peppers to your taste.

CREAM OF ROTEL SOUP

SERVES 3

½   small onion, chopped
⅛   cup finely chopped celery
2   teaspoons all-purpose flour
1   can (14½ ounces) fat-free chicken broth
1½ teaspoons Molly McButter butter sprinkles
¾   cup canned Rotel tomatoes
⅛   teaspoon garlic powder
    Salt and black pepper
½   teaspoon red pepper flakes (optional)
⅓   cup fat-free sour cream

Spray medium saucepan with nonstick cooking spray. Brown onion and celery over medium heat. Add flour and gradually add chicken broth until flour is mixed in and smooth. Add butter sprinkles, tomatoes, garlic powder, salt and pepper to taste, and red pepper flakes if desired. Simmer over low heat for about 15 minutes or until celery is cooked. Whisk in sour cream and serve.

Each serving provides:

65	Calories	1.1 g	Fiber
0.1 g	Fat	901 mg	Sodium
4.2 g	Protein	0 mg	Cholesterol
11.6 g	Carbohydrates		

Diabetic exchanges: Starch, ½; vegetable, 1

Pasta Spinach Salad

Serves 2

1   cup cooked pasta twists
1   cup lightly packed torn spinach leaves
2   green onions, chopped
½   medium cucumber, chopped
¼   medium green bell pepper, seeded and chopped
    Salt and black pepper
1   teaspoon sesame seeds
⅓   cup fat-free bottled ranch dressing
1   tablespoon salsa
1   clove garlic, pressed
1   tablespoon fat-free sour cream

In large bowl, combine pasta, spinach, green onions, cucumber, bell pepper, and salt and pepper to taste and toss.

To make dressing, spray small pan or skillet with nonstick cooking spray and brown sesame seeds over medium-low heat—about 1 minute or less—watch carefully, these burn very quickly. After browning, set aside to cool.

In small bowl, combine ranch dressing, salsa, garlic, and sour cream and mix. Add sesame seeds and mix. Pour dressing over salad and serve.

Each serving provides:

183	Calories	3.4 g	Fiber
1.5 g	Fat	549 mg	Sodium
5.9 g	Protein	0 mg	Cholesterol
34.9 g	Carbohydrates		

Diabetic exchanges: Starch, 2; vegetable, 1

Southwest Jalapeño Roasted Garlic

1   head of garlic
2   tablespoons white cooking wine
1   tablespoon Tabasco jalapeño sauce (green)
    Salt and black pepper
    Chili powder (optional)

Preheat oven to 375 degrees F.

Remove any extra outside layers from the head of garlic, but keep the entire head intact. Slice off about one-fourth of an inch from the top of the garlic head. Place head of garlic, sliced-side up, in very small ovenproof bowl. I use a bowl that is designed to roast garlic and that comes with a lid, but you can also cover the top of your dish with foil.

Pour wine into the center of the garlic head, followed by jalapeño sauce. Season with salt and pepper to taste and a little chili powder if desired. Place covered dish in oven for 45 minutes to 1 hour. Wonderful when served with any Mexican meal or dish.

Each serving provides:

15	Calories	0.2 g	Fiber
0.1 g	Fat	201 mg	Sodium
0.6 g	Protein	0 mg	Cholesterol
3.2 g	Carbohydrates		

Diabetic exchange: Vegetable, 1

Spicy Pasta Salad

1 cup cooked pasta
2 green onions, chopped
½ cup sliced or julienned carrots
½ cup canned or cooked brown beans, drained and rinsed
¼ bell pepper, seeded and chopped
1 small fresh tomato, chopped
1 tablespoon chopped fresh cilantro
  Salt and black pepper
½ cup fat-free sour cream
1 small clove garlic, pressed
  Juice of ½ fresh lime
½ teaspoon crushed red pepper flakes
  Dash of chili powder
  Pinch of ground cumin

In medium bowl, combine pasta, green onions, carrots, beans, bell pepper, tomato, cilantro, and salt and pepper to taste. Toss and mix. In small bowl, combine sour cream, garlic, lime juice, red pepper flakes, chili powder, and cumin. Stir and mix.

Pour dressing over pasta salad and chill slightly before serving.

Each serving provides:

161	Calories	4.1 g	Fiber
1 g	Fat	122 mg	Sodium
7.7 g	Protein	0 mg	Cholesterol
31.3 g	Carbohydrates		

Diabetic exchange: Starch, 2

Potato and Black Bean Soup

½ small onion, chopped
1 slice turkey bacon, cut into small pieces
1 small potato, peeled and cut into small chunks
1 cup fat-free chicken broth
½ cup frozen corn, thawed
1 cup drained canned green beans
1 cup water
½ cup drained canned black beans
   Salt and black pepper
3 tablespoons fat-free sour cream

Spray medium saucepan with nonstick cooking spray. Add onion and bacon pieces and brown over medium heat. Add potato, chicken broth, corn, green beans, water, black beans, and salt and pepper to taste and simmer over low heat for about 20 minutes. Whisk in sour cream and serve.

Each serving provides:

120	Calories	4.3 g	Fiber
1.2 g	Fat	632 mg	Sodium
7 g	Protein	3 mg	Cholesterol
22.4 g	Carbohydrates		

Diabetic exchange: Starch, 1½

Spicy Steak Soup

⅓   pound fajita-style sliced beef
    Salt and black pepper
½   cup Rotel tomatoes
1   small onion, chopped
½   cup ranch-style beans, rinsed and drained
1½ tablespoons dry ranch dressing mix
½   cup Campbell's 98 percent fat-free condensed cream
    of mushroom soup
1   can (14½ ounces) fat-free chicken broth
1   clove garlic, pressed
¼   cup fat-free sour cream

Spray medium saucepan with nonstick cooking spray. Brown beef strips over medium heat. Season with salt and pepper to taste. Add tomatoes, onion, beans, dressing mix, cream of mushroom soup, chicken broth, and garlic. Stir and simmer over low heat for 30 to 40 minutes. Whisk in sour cream and serve.

Each serving provides:

144	Calories	1.9 g	Fiber
4.1 g	Fat	1470 mg	Sodium
13.1 g	Protein	24 mg	Cholesterol
13.3 g	Carbohydrates		

Diabetic exchanges: Lean meat, 1; starch, ¾

FIESTA TORTILLA CORN CHOWDER

SERVES 3

1 small onion, chopped
1 can (14½ ounces) fat-free chicken broth
½ cup water
1 clove garlic, pressed
½ cup frozen corn, thawed
3 tablespoons fat-free sour cream
1 tablespoon Old El Paso lowfat cheese and salsa dip
   Salt and black pepper
2 corn tortillas, cut in strips

Spray medium saucepan with nonstick cooking spray. Add onion and brown over medium heat. Add chicken broth, water, garlic, and corn. Simmer over low heat for about 10 minutes. Using a whisk, blend in sour cream, cheese dip, and salt and pepper to taste. Simmer 1 minute. Add tortilla strips and stir. Serve.

Each serving provides:

105	Calories	2.2 g	Fiber
0.8 g	Fat	699 mg	Sodium
4.6 g	Protein	0 mg	Cholesterol
20.4 g	Carbohydrates		

Diabetic exchange: Starch, 1⅓

FESTIVE TACO CORN SALAD

SERVES 4

1 cup canned corn, drained
1 cup canned white hominy, drained
2 green onions, chopped
½ cup canned chili beans, drained
¼ cup seeded and chopped bell pepper
3 tablespoons chopped fresh cilantro
⅓ cup fat-free sour cream
¼ teaspoon taco seasoning
½ teaspoon dry ranch dressing mix

In medium bowl, combine corn, hominy, onions, chili beans, bell pepper, and cilantro. In small bowl, combine sour cream, taco seasoning, and dressing mix. Pour dressing over salad and chill about 1 hour before serving.

Each serving provides:

101	Calories	2.2 g	Fiber
0.6 g	Fat	456 mg	Sodium
5 g	Protein	0 mg	Cholesterol
20.4 g	Carbohydrates		

Diabetic exchange: Starch, 1⅓

Flautas

½ small onion, chopped
⅓ cup canned nonfat refried beans
1 clove garlic, pressed
½ teaspoon chili powder
⅛ teaspoon ground cumin
2 teaspoons chopped canned green chilies
2 fat-free flour tortillas each (6 to 7 inches in diameter)
¼ cup Sargento light grated Cheddar cheese
3 tablespoons fat-free sour cream (optional)

Preheat oven to 375 degrees F.

Spray small skillet with nonstick cooking spray. Add onion and brown over medium heat. Add refried beans, garlic, chili powder, cumin, and chilies. Stir together.

Divide this mixture in half and spread evenly over each tortilla. Sprinkle half the cheese on top of each. Add 1½ tablespoons sour cream to each, if desired. Roll each tortilla into a tube shape. Spray glass loaf pan with nonstick cooking spray. Place each flauta in dish.

Bake for 15 minutes. Garnish with additional fat-free sour cream if desired.

Each serving provides:

138	Calories	7.1 g	Fiber
2.7 g	Fat	403 mg	Sodium
8.5 g	Protein	5 mg	Cholesterol
23 g	Carbohydrates		

Diabetic exchanges: Lean meat, ½; vegetable, 1; starch, 1

EMPANADAS (LITTLE MEAT PIES)

SERVES 3 (2 PIES PER SERVING)

½ pound ground turkey breast
1 small onion, chopped
½ cup salsa
1 tablespoon raisins
1 tablespoon chopped toasted pine nuts
⅛ teaspoon ground cloves
⅛ teaspoon ground cumin
  Salt and black pepper
1 roll (6 biscuits) Pillsbury refrigerated biscuits

Preheat oven to 400 degrees F.

Spray medium skillet with nonstick cooking spray. Brown ground turkey and onion over medium heat. Add salsa, raisins, pine nuts, cloves, cumin, and salt and pepper to taste. Stir over medium heat until all moisture has cooked away. Set aside.

Roll out a biscuit to twice its size. Place one spoonful of meat mixture into center of dough; fold dough over and pinch edges. Repeat with remaining meat and biscuits. Spray baking sheet with nonstick cooking spray. Place empanadas on baking sheet and bake for 10 to 12 minutes or until golden brown.

Each serving provides:

252	Calories	1.4 g	Fiber
5.1 g	Fat	934 mg	Sodium
22.5 g	Protein	46 mg	Cholesterol
29.3 g	Carbohydrates		

Diabetic exchanges: Lean meat, 2; vegetable, ½; starch, 1½

Black Bean Chili Pasta Salad

½ pound ground chicken breast or turkey breast
1 small onion, chopped
2 cloves garlic, pressed
1 jalapeño pepper, seeded and chopped
1½ tablespoons William's chili seasoning
½ cup canned black beans, drained
1 cup chopped canned tomatoes
2 cups cooked spiral pasta
4 tablespoons Sargento light grated Cheddar cheese (optional)
4 tablespoons fat-free sour cream (optional)

Spray medium saucepan with nonstick cooking spray. Brown ground chicken and onion over medium heat. Add garlic, jalapeño pepper, chili seasoning, beans, and tomatoes. Simmer chili over low heat for 20 to 25 minutes.

Place pasta in four serving bowls and top with chili. Garnish with 1 tablespoon each of grated cheese and fat-free sour cream, if desired.

Each serving provides:

218	Calories	4 g	Fiber
1.6 g	Fat	212 mg	Sodium
18.2 g	Protein	30 mg	Cholesterol
31.8 g	Carbohydrates		

Diabetic exchanges: Lean meat, 1; starch, 2

Taco Cheese Soup

1 small onion, chopped
1 clove garlic, pressed
1 corn tortilla, cut into small pieces
1 can (14½ ounces) fat-free chicken broth
½ cup water
2 teaspoons taco seasoning
¼ cup Old El Paso lowfat cheese and salsa dip
3 tablespoons fat-free sour cream
   Black pepper

Spray medium saucepan with nonstick cooking spray. Add onion, garlic, and tortilla pieces. Stir and cook over low heat for 5 minutes. Add chicken broth, water, and taco seasoning. Add cheese dip and whisk until smooth. Add sour cream and whisk until smooth. Add black pepper to taste. Serve warm.

Each serving provides:

127	Calories	1.9 g	Fiber
2 g	Fat	1439 mg	Sodium
5.9 g	Protein	0 mg	Cholesterol
19.4 g	Carbohydrates		

Diabetic exchanges: Lean meat, ½; starch, 1

GREEN CHILI AND POSOLE STEW

SERVES 3

3 ounces very lean pork, cut into small chunks
1 small onion, chopped
1 cup hominy or posole
½ fresh green chili, seeded and sliced
1 can (14½ ounces) fat-free chicken broth
½ cup canned green chili enchilada sauce
1 clove garlic, pressed
1 very small potato, peeled and cut into small cubes
   Salt and black pepper
½ cup chopped or sliced carrots

Spray a medium to large saucepan with nonstick cooking spray. Add pork and onion. Brown over medium heat. Add hominy, green chili, chicken broth, enchilada sauce, garlic, potato, salt and pepper to taste, and carrots. Simmer over low heat for 35 to 45 minutes and serve.

Each serving provides:

152	Calories	1.9 g	Fiber
2.6 g	Fat	1004 mg	Sodium
9.4 g	Protein	15 mg	Cholesterol
22.7 g	Carbohydrates		

Diabetic exchanges: Lean meat, 1; vegetable, 1; starch, 1

Hot Creamy Onion Cheese Dip

Serves 6

½ cup Campbell's condensed cream of onion soup
1   clove garlic, pressed
4   tablespoons Old El Paso lowfat cheese and salsa dip
⅓ cup fat-free sour cream
⅓ cup fat-free chicken broth

Mix all ingredients in small saucepan and stir over low heat for 2 to 3 minutes. Serve warm with baked tortilla chips. Could also be used as a sauce over chicken.

Each serving provides:

39	Calories	0.2 g	Fiber
1.5 g	Fat	310 mg	Sodium
1.6 g	Protein	3 mg	Cholesterol
4.8 g	Carbohydrates		

Diabetic exchanges: Lean meat, ⅓; starch, ⅓

Black Bean Salsa Dip

1 can (15 ounces) black beans, drained
1 cup thick-and-chunky salsa
1 clove garlic, pressed
¼ cup chopped or shredded carrots
¾ cup fat-free sour cream
¼ teaspoon black pepper
  Dash of seasoned salt (optional)

Combine all ingredients in medium bowl and chill. Serve with baked tortilla chips.

Each serving provides:

76	Calories	3.5 g	Fiber
0.3 g	Fat	465 mg	Sodium
5.5 g	Protein	0 mg	Cholesterol
13.9 g	Carbohydrates		

Diabetic exchanges: Lean meat, ½; starch, ¾

Tasty Taco Rolls

Serves 3 (2 rolls per serving)

½ pound ground turkey breast or chicken breast
½ medium onion, chopped
2 tablespoons taco seasoning
¼ cup water
¼ teaspoon garlic powder
½ cup fat-free sour cream
1 egg white, slightly beaten
6 egg roll wrappers (usually found in the produce section)
  Garlic salt (optional)
  Black pepper (optional)

Preheat oven to 375 degrees F.

Spray large skillet with nonstick cooking spray. Brown ground turkey and onion over medium heat. Add taco seasoning, water, garlic powder, and sour cream. Stir and simmer over medium heat until all liquid is absorbed or cooked away. Set aside to cool.

Set out two dinner plates. Pour egg white onto one of them. Dip one side of an egg roll wrapper in egg white. Do not soak. Place egg roll wrapper, dipped side down, on other plate. Spoon about ⅙ cup of taco mixture onto the wrapper and roll up like an egg roll. Spray baking sheet with nonstick cooking spray. Place taco rolls on baking sheet. Sprinkle top of each roll with a little garlic salt and black pepper if desired. Repeat until all taco meat is used.

Bake for 20 to 25 minutes or until golden brown. Serve warm.

Each serving provides:

359	Calories	2.9 g	Fiber
1.4 g	Fat	627 mg	Sodium
30.6 g	Protein	46 mg	Cholesterol
57 g	Carbohydrates		

Diabetic exchanges: Lean meat, 2; starch, 3

CHEESE AND GREEN CHILI POCKETS

SERVES 5

½   cup corn flour

¼   cup water

1   egg white, slightly beaten

1½ slices fat-free mozzarella cheese, cut into 5 strips

1½ slices fat-free American or Cheddar cheese,
    cut into 5 strips

3   tablespoons chopped canned green chilies

½   small onion, chopped
    Garlic salt

Preheat oven to 375 degrees F.

In a bowl, mix corn flour and water, then add egg white and mix. Form dough into 5 balls. Place each dough ball between two sheets of wax paper and roll out to form a circle. Place 1 strip of each kind of cheese, a spoonful of green chilies, and a sprinkle of onions in the center of each circle. Fold in half and seal edges with a fork.

Spray baking sheet with nonstick cooking spray; set aside. Place each pocket on baking sheet and spray tops lightly with nonstick cooking spray to help browning. Sprinkle the top of each pocket lightly with garlic salt to taste. Bake for 35 to 40 minutes. Serve with salsa if desired.

These are so good! I love them.

Each serving provides:

62	Calories	0.8 g	Fiber
0.5 g	Fat	113 mg	Sodium
4.3 g	Protein	1 mg	Cholesterol
10.9 g	Carbohydrates		

Diabetic exchanges: Lean meat, ¼; starch, ⅔

Potato Skins with Green Chilies and Cheese

Serves 4

2 medium-size baking potatoes
½ cup fat-free sour cream
2 tablespoons chopped canned green chilies
4 green onions, chopped
¼ cup light Cheez Whiz
2 slices turkey bacon, cooked
   Garlic salt

Preheat oven to 400 degrees F.

Bake potatoes for about 1 hour. Remove from oven and allow to cool before handling. Slice each potato in half lengthwise and scoop out and discard center of each to make room for filling.

Spray baking pan or sheet with nonstick cooking spray. Into each potato half, spread 2 teaspoons sour cream, ½ tablespoon green chilies, ½ to 1 teaspoon green onions, and 1 tablespoon Cheez Whiz. Garnish each with ½ piece of turkey bacon, crumbled or broken into small pieces. Sprinkle each with garlic salt to taste.

Place potato halves on baking sheet. Bake for 10 to 12 minutes. Serve with salsa and/or fat-free sour cream. These disappeared in a matter of minutes when I made them—they were a huge hit with everyone.

Each serving provides:

141	Calories	1.7 g	Fiber
2.3 g	Fat	395 mg	Sodium
7.7 g	Protein	13 mg	Cholesterol
22.1 g	Carbohydrates		

Diabetic exchanges: Lean meat, 1; starch, 1

Southwest Bean Salad

¼ cup Miracle Whip fat-free dressing or
  fat-free mayonnaise
⅛ teaspoon chili powder
¼ teaspoon parsley flakes
½ teaspoon chopped chives
1 clove garlic, pressed, or ⅛ to ¼ teaspoon garlic powder
1 can (16 ounces) chili beans, rinsed and
  drained thoroughly
½ medium onion, chopped
⅛ cup chopped canned green chilies, drained
1 stalk celery, chopped
¼ cup seeded and chopped green or red bell pepper
½ tomato, chopped

In small bowl, combine Miracle Whip, chili powder, parsley flakes, chives, and garlic. In large bowl, combine chili beans, onion, chilies, celery, bell pepper, and tomato. Add dressing mixture and toss. Chill and serve.

Each serving provides:

104	Calories	2.9 g	Fiber
0.4 g	Fat	432 mg	Sodium
5.1 g	Protein	0 mg	Cholesterol
20.9 g	Carbohydrates		

Diabetic exchanges: Vegetable, 1; starch, 1

CRUNCHY MEXICAN FLATS

2   small corn or fat-free flour tortillas
1   egg white, slightly beaten
    Garlic salt
2   tablespoons (approximately) fat-free sour cream
2   tablespoons chopped onion
2   tablespoons chopped canned green chilies
¼   cup Mexican beans (optional)
¼   cup (approximately) light Cheez Whiz, warmed

Preheat oven to 400 degrees F.

Spray large baking sheet with nonstick cooking spray. Dip both sides of each tortilla in egg white. Do not soak. Place on baking sheet and sprinkle each tortilla with garlic salt to taste. Bake for 8 to 10 minutes. They will be lightly browned. Do not undercook, or they will not be crisp.

Remove from oven and spread each tortilla with 1 tablespoon sour cream, 1 tablespoon onion, 1 tablespoon green chilies, and beans if you wish. Drizzle each with 1 tablespoon Cheez Whiz. Return to oven and warm for 2 to 3 minutes. Remove and serve with salsa if desired.

These are so good. I like them better without the beans.

Each serving provides:

190	Calories	2.2 g	Fiber
3.7 g	Fat	649 mg	Sodium
11.7 g	Protein	15 mg	Cholesterol
25.8 g	Carbohydrates		

Diabetic exchanges: Lean meat, 1; vegetable, 2; starch, 1

Cheesy Nachos

SERVES 4

2 ounces light Velveeta
⅓ cup fat-free sour cream
⅓ cup salsa
5 cups baked tortilla chips
⅛ cup seeded and sliced jalapeño peppers (optional)
  Fat-free sour cream (optional)

Preheat oven to 400 degrees F.

In small saucepan, combine Velveeta, sour cream, and salsa. Stir over low heat until cheese is melted. Place chips in baking pan sprayed with nonstick cooking spray and heat in oven for 4 to 5 minutes. Remove; pour cheese mixture over chips and return to oven for 2 to 3 minutes. Remove from oven. Add jalapeño peppers and garnish with a few spoonfuls of fat-free sour cream if desired.

Each serving provides:

161	Calories	1.7 g	Fiber
2.5 g	Fat	380 mg	Sodium
6.4 g	Protein	5 mg	Cholesterol
28.1 g	Carbohydrates		

Diabetic exchanges: Lean meat, ¾; starch, 1½

Spicy Bean Dip

¾ cup canned fat-free refried beans
1 green onion, chopped
1 tablespoon chopped canned green chilies
¼ cup fat-free sour cream
¼ cup Sargento light grated Cheddar cheese
1 teaspoon taco seasoning
   Sliced jalapeño peppers, to taste (optional)

Preheat oven to 350 degrees F.

In medium bowl, combine refried beans, green onion, chilies, sour cream, cheese, and taco seasoning and mix. Spray small casserole with nonstick cooking spray. Pour mixture into casserole and top with sliced jalapeño peppers if desired. Bake for 20 to 25 minutes. Serve with no-oil tortilla chips.

Each serving provides:

124	Calories	4.7 g	Fiber
1.5 g	Fat	538 mg	Sodium
8.9 g	Protein	3 mg	Cholesterol
22 g	Carbohydrates		

Diabetic exchanges: Lean meat, ½; vegetable, 1; starch, 1

Santa Fe Chicken Soup

3 ounces boneless, skinless chicken breast, cut into small pieces
½ medium onion, chopped
½ stalk celery, chopped
1 can (14½ ounces) fat-free chicken broth
½ cup stewed, chopped tomatoes
½ clove garlic, pressed
2 tablespoons chopped canned green chilies
1 teaspoon taco seasoning
¼ cup fat-free sour cream
3 corn tortillas, cut into 1-inch pieces

Spray large pot with nonstick cooking spray. Brown chicken pieces over medium heat. Add onion and celery and continue cooking until brown. Add chicken broth, tomatoes, garlic, chilies, and taco seasoning and simmer over medium-low heat for 15 minutes.

Add sour cream and simmer over low heat for 1 to 2 minutes. Add tortillas and simmer 1 to 2 minutes. Serve.

Each serving provides:

150	Calories	2.7 g	Fiber
1.1 g	Fat	882 mg	Sodium
11.6 g	Protein	16 mg	Cholesterol
22.6 g	Carbohydrates		

Diabetic exchanges: Lean meat, 1; vegetable, 1; starch, 1

Chicken Taco Salad

½ pound boneless, skinless chicken breasts, cut into
    small pieces
1 tablespoon taco seasoning
¼ cup taco sauce
1 teaspoon dry onion flakes
½ cup canned whole kernel corn, drained
2 tablespoons chopped canned green chilies
¼ cup fat-free sour cream
½ teaspoon dry ranch dressing mix
    Buns or sandwich bagels (optional)

Spray skillet with nonstick cooking spray. Add chicken pieces and brown over medium heat for 4 to 6 minutes. Sprinkle with taco seasoning and stir over medium heat for 1 to 2 minutes. Add taco sauce and onion flakes and stir. Reduce heat to low and simmer until all liquid is cooked into meat. Remove from heat and let cool.

In medium bowl, combine chicken, corn, chilies, sour cream, and dressing mix. Stir until thoroughly mixed and chill for a few hours before serving.

Serve on a bun or bagel as a sandwich. Can be rolled in flour or corn tortilla or served on a lettuce leaf and garnished with chopped tomatoes and grated light cheese.

Each serving provides:

156	Calories	1.7 g	Fiber
1.5 g	Fat	722 mg	Sodium
20.4 g	Protein	44 mg	Cholesterol
12 g	Carbohydrates		

Diabetic exchanges: Lean meat, 2; vegetable, 2

ZESTY LAYERED DIP

SERVES 4

½ pound ground turkey breast or chicken breast
1 tablespoon taco seasoning
¼ cup water
¾ cup fat-free refried beans
3 tablespoons chopped canned green chilies
½ small onion, chopped
1 cup fat-free sour cream
½ cup Sargento light grated Cheddar cheese
1 large tomato, chopped (optional)

Spray skillet with nonstick cooking spray. Brown ground turkey over medium heat. Add taco seasoning and water. Simmer and stir over low heat until all water is cooked away. Set aside to cool.

Spread refried beans evenly over bottom of 8-inch square baking dish. Layer with meat, chilies, onion, and sour cream. Top with grated cheese and tomato if desired. Chill and serve with no-oil tortilla chips.

Each serving provides:

202	Calories	3.3 g	Fiber
3.3 g	Fat	687 mg	Sodium
24.6 g	Protein	39 mg	Cholesterol
20.3 g	Carbohydrates		

Diabetic exchanges: Lean meat, 2; vegetable, ½; starch, 1

CREAMY MEXICAN SOUP

SERVES 3

1 slice turkey bacon, cut into small pieces
1 small onion, chopped
¾ cup fat-free chicken broth
1 can (16 ounces) golden hominy, drained
1 cup water
2 tablespoons chopped canned green chilies
1 clove garlic, pressed
  Black pepper
¼ cup fat-free sour cream

Spray saucepan with nonstick cooking spray. Brown bacon and onion over medium heat. Add chicken broth, hominy, water, chilies, garlic, and black pepper to taste and simmer over medium heat about 20 minutes.

Stir in sour cream just before serving.

Each serving provides:

98	Calories	1.4 g	Fiber
0.9 g	Fat	576 mg	Sodium
4.3 g	Protein	3 mg	Cholesterol
18 g	Carbohydrates		

Diabetic exchanges: Lean meat, ¼; starch, 1

QUESO WITH GREEN CHILIES

½ cup Sargento light grated Cheddar cheese
⅓ cup green chili enchilada sauce
¼ cup chopped stewed tomatoes
2 tablespoons chopped canned green chilies
1 teaspoon dry onion flakes
1 clove garlic, pressed, or ⅛ teaspoon garlic powder

In food processor, blend cheese and enchilada sauce until smooth. Transfer to saucepan and combine with tomatoes, chilies, onion flakes, and garlic and simmer over very low heat for 2 to 4 minutes, until heated (see note). Serve warm with no-oil tortilla chips.

Each serving provides:

59	Calories	0.4 g	Fiber
3.2 g	Fat	312 mg	Sodium
4.3 g	Protein	5 mg	Cholesterol
4.4 g	Carbohydrates		

Diabetic exchanges: Lean meat, ½; vegetable, 1

Note: Be sure to warm the cheese mixture over very low heat. If heat is too high, cheese will separate and curdle.

Mexican Cheese and Chicken Rolls

2 boneless, skinless chicken breasts (2 to 3 ounces each), cut into long strips
2 egg roll wrappers
1 egg white, slightly beaten
2 tablespoons chopped green chilies
½ cup Sargento light grated Cheddar cheese
   Salt (optional)

Preheat oven to 350 degrees F.

Spray medium skillet with nonstick cooking spray. Add chicken and cook over medium heat for 3 to 4 minutes, until almost done. (The chicken will finish cooking in the oven.)

Dip one side of an egg roll wrapper in egg white. The dipped side will be the outside of the roll. Place 3 to 4 strips of chicken just below the center of the wrapper. Sprinkle 1 to 2 tablespoons green chilies on top. Top with ¼ cup cheese. Season with a little salt if desired and roll up like an egg roll. (Directions are on the back of the egg roll wrapper package if needed.) Repeat for second egg roll. Spray baking sheet with nonstick cooking spray. Place rolls on baking sheet and bake for 20 to 25 minutes or until golden brown.

Each serving provides:

230	Calories	0.7 g	Fiber
5.6 g	Fat	325 mg	Sodium
31.5 g	Protein	59 mg	Cholesterol
14.1 g	Carbohydrates		

Diabetic exchanges: Lean meat, 3; starch, 1

Southwest Tossed Salad

Serves 4

3 cups lettuce
½ cup fresh spinach
2 radishes, sliced
1 medium tomato, chopped
1 small purple onion, chopped
1 jalapeño pepper, seeded and sliced (use green chilies
   for a milder taste)
½ cup Sargento light grated Cheddar cheese
1 teaspoon chopped fresh cilantro
1 cup chunky salsa
4 tablespoons fat-free sour cream

In large bowl, combine lettuce, spinach, radishes, tomato,
onion, jalapeño pepper, cheese, and cilantro and toss gently.
In small bowl, combine salsa and sour cream and mix. Pour
dressing over salad just before serving.

Each serving provides:

87	Calories	2.8 g	Fiber
2.8 g	Fat	592 mg	Sodium
7 g	Protein	5 mg	Cholesterol
10.7 g	Carbohydrates		

Diabetic exchanges: Lean meat, ½; vegetable, 2

CHEESE SOUP WITH GREEN CHILIES

SERVES 2

2   cups tomato juice
2   tablespoons chopped canned green chilies
⅛   cup finely chopped onion
½   clove garlic, pressed
2½   tablespoons Sargento light grated Cheddar cheese
     Dash of Tabasco sauce
     Dash of seasoned salt
     Chopped parsley for garnish (optional)

Heat tomato juice over medium heat in saucepan for 2 to 3 minutes. Add chilies, onion, garlic, cheese, Tabasco, and seasoned salt and simmer over low heat until cheese is melted. Stir constantly. Serve hot and garnish with a little chopped parsley and a sprinkle of light cheese if desired.

Each serving provides:

73	Calories	1.4 g	Fiber
1.6 g	Fat	975 mg	Sodium
4.7 g	Protein	3 mg	Cholesterol
12.8 g	Carbohydrates		

Diabetic exchanges: Lean meat, ½; vegetable, 2

WESTERN CORN CHOWDER

½ small onion, chopped
¼ cup fat-free sour cream
½ cup fat-free chicken broth
½ cup canned evaporated skim milk
1½ slices turkey bacon, cooked and chopped
1 cup drained whole kernel corn
½ cup water
⅛ teaspoon Molly McButter butter sprinkles
¼ teaspoon celery flakes
¼ cup Sargento light grated Cheddar cheese
   Salt and black pepper

Spray saucepan with nonstick cooking spray. Brown onion over medium heat until golden brown. Remove from heat and add sour cream. Stir while gradually adding chicken broth and milk. Return to medium heat and add bacon, corn, water, butter sprinkles, celery flakes, cheese, and salt and pepper to taste. Simmer over very low heat for 5 to 10 minutes, stirring often. Serve.

Each serving provides:

105	Calories	0.9 g	Fiber
2.2 g	Fat	397 mg	Sodium
8 g	Protein	8 mg	Cholesterol
15.1 g	Carbohydrates		

Diabetic exchanges: Lean meat, ½; starch, 1

Queso Cheese Dip

SERVES 4

½ cup Sargento light grated Cheddar cheese
½ cup Campbell's 98 percent fat-free condensed cream
   of mushroom soup
1 tablespoon finely chopped onion
¼ cup chopped fresh tomatoes
½ tablespoon chopped canned green chilies
2 tablespoons fat-free sour cream
½ cup water

Combine all ingredients in saucepan and simmer over very
low heat until cheese has melted. Serve hot with any lowfat
cracker or oil-free tortilla chips or pretzels. Great for a party.

Each serving provides:

58	Calories	0.1 g	Fiber
2.8 g	Fat	228 mg	Sodium
4.9 g	Protein	6 mg	Cholesterol
4.1 g	Carbohydrates		

Diabetic exchanges: Lean meat, ½; vegetable, 1

CHILI CHEESE DIP

SERVES 3

1 cup canned turkey chili
3 tablespoons fat-free sour cream
¼ cup water
½ cup Sargento light grated Cheddar cheese
  Onions, jalapeño peppers, or green chilies to taste
  (optional)

In small saucepan, combine chili, sour cream, water, and cheese. Stir over low heat until cheese is thoroughly melted. If you wish, add chopped fresh onions, chopped jalapeño peppers, or chopped green chilies to taste. Serve as a dip with reduced-fat tortilla chips. Great for a party.

Each serving provides:

126	Calories	1.3 g	Fiber
4.3 g	Fat	471 mg	Sodium
12.6 g	Protein	22 mg	Cholesterol
10.7 g	Carbohydrates		

Diabetic exchanges: Lean meat, 1; vegetable, 1; starch, ½

Green Chili Quesadillas

½ cup Sargento light grated Cheddar cheese
2 small soft flour tortillas
¼ cup chopped green onion
¼ cup chopped canned green chilies

Preheat oven to 375 degrees F.

Sprinkle ¼ cup cheese onto half of each flour tortilla. Place half of the green onion and green chilies on each. Fold the empty half over the filled half, to form a half moon. Spray a baking sheet with nonstick cooking spray. Place quesadillas on baking sheet and bake for 20 to 25 minutes. Serve warm.

May be sliced into pie-shaped sections and garnished with fat-free sour cream, chopped tomatoes, salsa, etc. Makes a great appetizer for parties.

Each serving provides:

173	Calories	1.4 g	Fiber
6.3 g	Fat	273 mg	Sodium
10.7 g	Protein	10 mg	Cholesterol
20.1 g	Carbohydrates		

Diabetic exchanges: Lean meat, 1; vegetable, 1; starch, 1

CRISPY CHEESE TORTILLAS

SERVES 2

2 small corn tortillas
¼ cup Sargento light grated Cheddar cheese
   Garlic salt
2 tablespoons fat-free sour cream

Preheat oven to 375 degrees F.

Spray baking sheet with nonstick cooking spray. Place tortillas on baking sheet and place in oven. *Watch carefully—tortillas burn easily!* Bake about 2 minutes and remove. Sprinkle half the cheese on each tortilla, sprinkle on garlic salt to taste, and return to oven for about 2 minutes. Serve with fat-free sour cream on the side.

Each serving provides:

112	Calories	1.6 g	Fiber
2.9 g	Fat	163 mg	Sodium
6.5 g	Protein	5 mg	Cholesterol
15.5 g	Carbohydrates		

Diabetic exchanges: Lean meat, ⅔; starch, 1

2

MAIN DISHES

Southwest Skillet Dinner

2   boneless, skinless chicken breasts (3 ounces each)
⅛ cup Allegro marinade (bottled liquid marinade)
1   small onion, chopped
1   medium potato, cut into small chunks
    Salt and black pepper
½ cup salsa

Place chicken breasts in small dish containing marinade. Cover and place in refrigerator to marinate for 2 to 3 hours. Discard marinade.

Spray medium skillet with nonstick cooking spray. Add chicken and brown over low heat. Add onion, potato, and salt and pepper to taste. Simmer and cook until potatoes are browned and done. Add salsa and simmer 1 to 2 minutes. Serve.

Each serving provides:

167	Calories	2.6 g	Fiber
1.4 g	Fat	791 mg	Sodium
21.9 g	Protein	49 mg	Cholesterol
16.8 g	Carbohydrates		

Diabetic exchanges: Lean meat, 2; vegetable, 1; starch, ½

CHALUPAS

1   pound (4 to 5) boneless pork loin chops
     Salt and black pepper
2   cups water
1   can (15 ounces) ranch-style beans, rinsed and drained
1   can (4½ ounces) green chilies, chopped
1   can (8 ounces) tomato sauce
1   teaspoon chili powder
½   teaspoon ground cumin
½   teaspoon garlic salt
     Baked tortilla chips

Spray a large pan with a tight-fitting cover, such as a Dutch oven, with nonstick cooking spray. Season pork chops with salt and pepper. Place pork chops in prepared pan over medium-high heat. Brown on both sides, then reduce heat to low and pour 1 cup water over pork. Cover pan tightly and simmer over low heat for 1 hour or until tender. Add 1 cup water at the end of cooking time, when liquid has cooked down.

Remove pork chops to a plate to cool. Save the liquid in the pan and add beans, chilies, tomato sauce, chili powder, cumin, and garlic salt, stirring to blend.

Shred or cut pork into very small pieces and return to pan, stirring into mixture. Simmer over low heat for 10 to 15 minutes.

To serve, make a bed of baked tortilla chips on each of four plates. Spoon ½ cup of the pork mixture on top of the chips. Top with desired toppings, such as shredded lettuce, chopped tomatoes, chopped onions, grated lowfat cheese, and fat-free sour cream.

This mixture is also good rolled up in a flour tortilla or served alone as chili.

Each serving provides:

279	Calories	6.2 g	Fiber
8 g	Fat	846 mg	Sodium
31.1 g	Protein	63 mg	Cholesterol
22.2 g	Carbohydrates		

Diabetic exchanges: Lean meat, 3; vegetable, 1; starch, 1

SOUTH-OF-THE-BORDER TURKEY LOAF

SERVES 6

1 pound ground turkey breast
½ cup chopped onion
½ cup seeded and chopped bell pepper
1 tablespoon seeded and chopped Anaheim pepper
¼ cup fat-free liquid egg product
½ cup cornflake crumbs
¼ cup salsa
2 tablespoons chopped fresh cilantro or parsley
1 teaspoon minced garlic
½ teaspoon salt
¼ teaspoon pepper

Preheat oven to 350 degrees F.

In large bowl, mix all ingredients together. Spray a loaf pan with nonstick cooking spray. Press mixture into loaf pan. Bake for 40 minutes.

Each serving provides:

165	Calories	0.9 g	Fiber
4.5 g	Fat	405 mg	Sodium
19.4 g	Protein	44 mg	Cholesterol
11.2 g	Carbohydrates		

Diabetic exchanges: Lean meat, 2; vegetable, ½; starch, ½

MEATY ZESTY CHILI

1   pound ground turkey breast
1   cup chopped onion
2   slices turkey bacon, chopped into small bits
2   tablespoons seeded and chopped fresh serrano or
    jalapeño pepper
1   can (14½ ounces) beef broth
1   can (14½ ounces) diced tomatoes
1   can (16 ounces) chili-flavored beans
1   can (8 ounces) tomato sauce
1   tablespoon chili powder
½   teaspoon salt
½   teaspoon garlic salt
1   teaspoon vinegar from pickled jalapeños

Spray a large cooking pan with nonstick cooking spray. Add
ground turkey, onion, and turkey bacon and sauté over medium heat, stirring often, for 2 to 3 minutes, until meat
is cooked.

Add chopped pepper, beef broth, tomatoes, beans, tomato sauce, chili powder, salt, garlic salt, and vinegar and simmer over low heat for 5 to 10 minutes. As with any chili, this is even better the next day!

Each serving provides:

214	Calories	5.8 g	Fiber
2.5 g	Fat	1668 mg	Sodium
26.3 g	Protein	51 mg	Cholesterol
23.6 g	Carbohydrates		

Diabetic exchanges: Lean meat, 2; vegetable, 1; starch, 1

Mexican Breakfast Sweet Onion Quiche

1 cup fat-free liquid egg product
1 small sweet onion, chopped
2 tablespoons seeded and chopped bell pepper
¼ cup frozen chopped spinach, drained and squeezed
½ cup Sargento light grated four-cheese Mexican cheese
1 tablespoon chopped canned green chilies
2 tablespoons fat-free sour cream
Salt and black pepper
1 (9-inch) frozen Pet Ritz pie crust

Preheat oven to 350 degrees F.

In medium bowl, combine egg product, onion, bell pepper, spinach, cheese, chilies, sour cream, and salt and pepper to taste. Mix thoroughly.

While the pie crust is still frozen, pop it out of its aluminum pie plate and place it in a 9-inch glass pie plate sprayed with cooking spray.

Pour quiche filling into unbaked pie crust and bake for 45 to 50 minutes.

Each serving provides:

162	Calories	0.5 g	Fiber
6.9 g	Fat	231 mg	Sodium
8.8 g	Protein	7 mg	Cholesterol
15.3 g	Carbohydrates		

Diabetic exchanges: Lean meat, 1; vegetable, 1; starch, 1

Southwest Grilled Steaks

2 very lean beef filet steaks (3 to 4 ounces each)
¼ cup Allegro hickory smoke marinade (bottled
   liquid marinade)
1 small onion, sliced
1 clove garlic, pressed
2 teaspoons Tabasco jalapeño sauce (green)

Place all ingredients in a large Ziploc bag. Seal and marinate for 3 to 4 hours in refrigerator. Turn every once in a while.

Discard marinade. Cook to taste on a grill (I like to cook them on an outdoor grill) and serve.

Each serving provides:

233	Calories	0 g	Fiber
10.7 g	Fat	397 mg	Sodium
31.9 g	Protein	94 mg	Cholesterol
0.1 g	Carbohydrates		

Diabetic exchange: Lean meat, 4⅓

Mexican Scrambled Eggs

½ cup fat-free liquid egg product
1 green onion, chopped
1 teaspoon chopped fresh cilantro
1 tablespoon seeded and chopped red bell pepper
  Garlic salt and black pepper
¼ teaspoon Molly McButter butter sprinkles
1 small tomato, chopped

Spray medium skillet with nonstick cooking spray. In small bowl, combine all ingredients. Pour into skillet, stir, and cook over medium heat for 2 to 4 minutes. Serve warm.

Each serving provides:

89	Calories	1.6 g	Fiber
0.4 g	Fat	256 mg	Sodium
13.1 g	Protein	0 mg	Cholesterol
8.3 g	Carbohydrates		

Diabetic exchanges: Lean meat, 1; vegetable, 1½

Paprika Chicken, Southwest Style

2 boneless, skinless chicken breasts (3 ounces each)
¼ teaspoon paprika
¼ teaspoon chili powder
¼ teaspoon garlic powder
  Salt and black pepper
1 small onion, chopped
½ cup fat-free sour cream
  Jalapeño peppers, seeded and sliced, to taste (optional)

Season each chicken breast with ⅛ teaspoon each of paprika, chili powder, and garlic powder, and add salt and pepper to taste. Spray medium skillet with nonstick cooking spray. Add chicken and onion to skillet and brown over low heat. Add sour cream and jalapeño peppers, if desired, and stir. Simmer over low heat for 5 to 10 minutes or until chicken is done. Serve.

Each serving provides:

116	Calories	0.9 g	Fiber
1.2 g	Fat	62 mg	Sodium
20.6 g	Protein	49 mg	Cholesterol
4.6 g	Carbohydrates		

Diabetic exchange: Lean meat, 2

CITRUS CHICKEN BREASTS

2 boneless, skinless chicken breasts (3 ounces each)
   Garlic powder
   Onion powder
   Salt and black pepper
   Juice of ½ fresh lime
   Juice of ½ fresh lemon
1 tablespoon frozen orange juice concentrate
½ teaspoon grated orange peel
½ cup fat-free chicken broth
1 tablespoon seeded and chopped bell pepper
¼ teaspoon red pepper flakes
1 tablespoon cornstarch

Spray small skillet with nonstick cooking spray. Season both sides of each chicken breast with garlic powder, onion powder, salt, and pepper to taste. Add chicken to skillet and brown, then cook over medium-low heat until done.

In small pan, combine lime juice, lemon juice, orange juice concentrate, orange peel, chicken broth, bell pepper, red pepper flakes, and cornstarch. Stir over medium heat until sauce thickens slightly. Pour sauce over chicken to serve.

Each serving provides:

134	Calories	0.5 g	Fiber
1.1 g	Fat	308 mg	Sodium
20.6 g	Protein	49 mg	Cholesterol
10 g	Carbohydrates		

Diabetic exchanges: Lean meat, 2; vegetable, 1

Chili Burgers

⅓ pound extra-lean ground beef
½ small onion, chopped
½ teaspoon chili powder
1 clove garlic, pressed
1 tablespoon dry rolled oats
1 tablespoon fat-free liquid egg product
½ fresh green chili pepper, seeded and chopped
   Dash of ground cumin
   Dash of Tabasco sauce
   Salt and black pepper

In medium bowl, combine ground beef, onion, chili powder, garlic, rolled oats, egg product, chili pepper, cumin, Tabasco, and salt and pepper to taste. Mix thoroughly and form into 2 patties. These can be cooked on the charcoal grill or in a skillet on top of the stove. (Charcoal-grilled is better, if you have time.)

Cook to desired doneness (I usually cook at least 4 to 5 minutes on each side). Serve on lowfat hamburger buns with mustard, lettuce, tomato, onion, or any other desired toppings.

Each serving provides:

184	Calories	1.1 g	Fiber
10.2 g	Fat	64 mg	Sodium
17.1 g	Protein	50 mg	Cholesterol
5.4 g	Carbohydrates		

Diabetic exchanges: Medium meat, 2; vegetable, 1

Southwest Cheesy Cornbread Casserole

1 small zucchini, sliced
1 small onion, sliced
½ cup grated carrot
1 small tomato, sliced
1 small yellow crookneck squash, sliced
¼ cup Sargento light grated Cheddar cheese
   Garlic salt
   Black pepper
1 tablespoon Molly McButter butter sprinkles
½ cup skim milk
1 fresh green chili pepper, seeded and chopped
¼ cup all-purpose flour
¾ cup cornmeal
2 packets Sweet 'n Low sweetener
3 tablespoons Equal sweetener
1½ teaspoons baking powder
¼ teaspoon salt
¼ cup fat-free liquid egg product
1 teaspoon olive oil

Preheat oven to 375 degrees F.

Spray an 8 × 8-inch glass baking dish with nonstick cooking spray. Layer bottom of dish with zucchini, onion, carrot, tomato, squash, and cheese. Season with garlic salt and black pepper to taste. Sprinkle vegetable layer with butter sprinkles.

To make cornbread topping: In medium bowl, combine milk, chili pepper, flour, cornmeal, sweeteners, baking powder, salt, egg product, and olive oil. Pour cornbread mixture over sliced vegetables and bake for 20 to 30 minutes.

Each serving provides:

219	Calories	3.8 g	Fiber
3.1 g	Fat	581 mg	Sodium
10.2 g	Protein	3 mg	Cholesterol
38.8 g	Carbohydrates		

Diabetic exchanges: Lean meat, 1; starch, 2

Mexican Frittata

1 small potato, peeled and cut into cubes
½ small onion, chopped
2 slices turkey bacon, cut into small pieces
¼ cup salsa
¾ cup fat-free liquid egg product
   Garlic salt
   Black pepper
¼ cup Sargento light grated four-cheese Mexican cheese

Preheat oven to 400 degrees F.

Spray medium skillet with nonstick cooking spray. Add potato, onion, and bacon. Stir and brown over low heat until onion and potato are tender. Add salsa and simmer until any juice from the salsa is gone. Spray a 9-inch pie plate with nonstick cooking spray. Transfer potato mixture to pie plate.

In small bowl, combine egg product, garlic salt and black pepper to taste, add cheese, and mix. Pour over potato mixture and bake for about 15 minutes or until egg is set. Garnish with ground red chili pepper if desired. Cut in pie-shaped pieces.

Each serving provides:

85	Calories	1 g	Fiber
2.5 g	Fat	338 mg	Sodium
8.6 g	Protein	8 mg	Cholesterol
7.7 g	Carbohydrates		

Diabetic exchanges: Lean meat, 1; vegetable, 1½

Mexican Lasagna

SERVES 4

⅓   pound extra-lean ground beef
1   small onion, chopped
1   clove garlic, pressed
3½ teaspoons taco seasoning
⅓   cup water
1   jalapeño pepper, seeded and sliced (optional)
4   soft corn tortillas
½   cup canned black beans, rinsed and drained
½   cup corn, fresh or frozen (if frozen, thawed)
½   cup salsa
½   cup fat-free cottage cheese
⅓   cup Sargento light grated Cheddar cheese

Preheat oven to 350 degrees F.

Spray medium skillet with nonstick cooking spray. Add ground beef, onion, and garlic and brown over medium heat. Add taco seasoning, water, and jalapeño pepper. Stir over low heat for 2 to 3 minutes.

Spray a glass loaf pan with nonstick cooking spray. Place two tortillas on the bottom of pan. Add alternate layers of meat mixture, beans, corn, salsa, cottage cheese, and remaining tortillas. Top with cheese. Bake for 20 to 25 minutes.

Each serving provides:

271	Calories	5 g	Fiber
8.9 g	Fat	743 mg	Sodium
18.2 g	Protein	32 mg	Cholesterol
28.9 g	Carbohydrates		

Diabetic exchanges: Lean meat, 2; starch, 2

Mouthwatering Southwest Meatballs

Serves 3 (about 5 meatballs per serving)

½ pound ground turkey breast
1 clove garlic, pressed
½ small onion, chopped
1 tablespoon seeded and finely chopped
   green bell pepper
   Salt and black pepper
½ teaspoon chili powder
1 tablespoon fat-free liquid egg product
½ cup jarred red chili sauce
1 tablespoon dry onion flakes
1 clove garlic, pressed
1 cup fat-free chicken broth
¼ cup white cooking wine

In medium bowl, combine ground turkey, garlic, onion, green pepper, salt and pepper to taste, chili powder, and egg product and mix thoroughly. Form into balls about the size of small walnuts. Place in skillet sprayed with nonstick cooking spray and brown over medium heat.

In medium bowl, combine chili sauce, onion flakes, garlic, chicken broth, and wine. Transfer sauce and meatballs to saucepan and simmer for 25 to 30 minutes. Serve warm, or chill and serve later reheated in a Crock-Pot.

Each serving provides:

143	Calories	1.1 g	Fiber
1.2 g	Fat	1003 mg	Sodium
16.3 g	Protein	36 mg	Cholesterol
15.1 g	Carbohydrates		

Diabetic exchanges: Lean meat, 2; starch, ½

FAJITAS WITH CHICKEN AND CUCUMBER

1 bell pepper, seeded and cut into chunks
1 medium onion, sliced
¼ cup fat-free chicken broth
2 boneless, skinless chicken breasts (3 ounces each),
   cooked on grill
4 small flour tortillas
1 medium cucumber, sliced lengthwise into several pieces
   Fat-free sour cream, fat-free cheese, and salsa for
   garnish (optional)

Spray medium skillet with nonstick cooking spray. Add bell
pepper, onion, and chicken broth. Brown and simmer over
medium heat. Set aside.

Slice cooked chicken breasts into long, slender pieces. In each tortilla, place some chicken, cucumber, pepper, and onion and roll up.

These are great garnished with fat-free sour cream, salsa, and fat-free cheese, if desired.

Each serving provides:

194	Calories	2.4 g	Fiber
3.5 g	Fat	149 mg	Sodium
16.7 g	Protein	37 mg	Cholesterol
23.4 g	Carbohydrates		

Diabetic exchanges: Lean meat, 1; vegetable, 2; starch, 1

SANTA FE CHICKEN BREASTS

2 boneless, skinless chicken breasts (3 ounces each)
 Salt and black pepper
 Chili powder
¼ cup Old El Paso lowfat cheese and salsa dip
½ small onion, chopped
1 cup fat-free chicken broth
1 teaspoon taco seasoning
⅓ cup water
3 tablespoons fat-free sour cream
1 clove garlic, pressed

Spray small skillet with nonstick cooking spray. Season chicken breasts with salt, pepper, and chili powder to taste. Place chicken breasts in skillet and brown over medium heat. Cook over medium-low heat for 3 to 4 minutes, until done.

In small pan, mix cheese dip, onion, chicken broth, taco seasoning, water, sour cream, and garlic. Stir and simmer over very low heat for 3 to 4 minutes. Do not boil. Pour this mixture over chicken in skillet and simmer for 1 to 2 minutes.

Each serving provides:

197	Calories	2.5 g	Fiber
3.1 g	Fat	2029 mg	Sodium
24.9 g	Protein	49 mg	Cholesterol
16.8 g	Carbohydrates		

Diabetic exchanges: Lean meat, 3; vegetable, 1

Tasty Taco Corn Flats

SERVES 4

½   pound extra-lean ground beef
1   teaspoon taco seasoning
⅓   cup water
2   green onions, chopped
4   soft corn tortillas
¼   cup fat-free liquid egg product
4   tablespoons Sargento light grated four-cheese
     Mexican cheese

Preheat oven to 350 degrees F.

Spray medium skillet with nonstick cooking spray. Brown and cook ground beef over medium heat for 4 to 6 minutes, until done. Add taco seasoning, water, and green onions and cook for 2 to 3 minutes. Set aside to cool.

Spray 9 × 9-inch baking dish with nonstick cooking spray. Line bottom of dish with corn tortillas. Stir egg product into meat mixture and pour on top of tortillas. Top with cheese. Bake for 20 to 25 minutes.

Each serving provides:

228	Calories	1.8 g	Fiber
11.4 g	Fat	223 mg	Sodium
15.7 g	Protein	42 mg	Cholesterol
14.8 g	Carbohydrates		

Diabetic exchanges: Lean meat, 2; vegetable, 1½; starch, 1

Skillet Mushroom-Garlic Chicken

Serves 2

2 boneless, skinless chicken breasts (3 ounces each)
2 tablespoons all-purpose flour
  Chili powder
  Garlic powder
  Onion powder
½ cup Campbell's 98 percent fat-free condensed cream
  of mushroom soup
½ cup fat-free chicken broth
2 tablespoons fat-free sour cream

Spray medium skillet with nonstick cooking spray. Dust each chicken breast on both sides with 1 tablespoon flour and place in skillet. Season chicken with chili powder, garlic powder, and onion powder to taste. Brown on both sides over medium heat.

In small bowl, whisk together cream of mushroom soup, chicken broth, and sour cream. Mix thoroughly. Pour over chicken and simmer over low heat for about 12 minutes.

Each serving provides:

166	Calories	0.2 g	Fiber
2.1 g	Fat	557 mg	Sodium
22.5 g	Protein	51 mg	Cholesterol
12.5 g	Carbohydrates		

Diabetic exchanges: Lean meat, 2; starch, ¾

BLACKENED RED CHILI CHICKEN BREASTS

SERVES 2

2 boneless, skinless chicken breasts (3 ounces each)
½ teaspoon chili powder (approximately)
¼ teaspoon onion powder (approximately)
¼ teaspoon garlic powder (approximately)
¼ teaspoon black pepper (approximately)
1 fresh green chili pepper, seeded and cut in
   half lengthwise

Season each chicken breast on both sides with ¼ teaspoon chili powder and ⅛ teaspoon each of onion powder, garlic powder, and black pepper. Spray small skillet with nonstick cooking spray. Place chicken breasts in skillet.

Place chili pepper in skillet to cook and brown with chicken over medium heat. Cover and cook over low heat for 10 to 15 minutes or until chicken is done. Serve each chicken breast with a pepper half.

Each serving provides:

156	Calories	0.7 g	Fiber
3.2 g	Fat	71 mg	Sodium
27.3 g	Protein	73 mg	Cholesterol
3.1 g	Carbohydrates		

Diabetic exchange: Lean meat, 3

CRUNCHY TOSTITO CHICKEN

SERVES 2

2 tablespoons fat-free sour cream
  Juice of ½ lime
1 clove garlic, pressed
  Dash of chili powder
2 boneless, skinless chicken breasts (3 ounces each)
½ cup crushed Baked Tostitos tortilla chips
  (approximately)
  Salt and black pepper

Preheat oven to 350 degrees F.

In small bowl, combine sour cream, lime juice, garlic, and chili powder. Mix well. Dip each chicken breast in sour cream mixture and then roll or press in crushed tortilla chips. Spray 8-inch baking dish with nonstick cooking spray. Place chicken breasts in baking dish. Season chicken with salt and pepper to taste. Bake for 25 to 35 minutes.

Each serving provides:

217	Calories	1.5 g	Fiber
2.9 g	Fat	52 mg	Sodium
20.1 g	Protein	47 mg	Cholesterol
26 g	Carbohydrates		

Diabetic exchanges: Lean meat, 2; vegetable, 1; starch, 1

Mexican Corn and Pepperoni Pizza

Serves 2

⅓ cup mild salsa
1 (7-inch) Mama Mary's pizza crust or other lowfat ready-
   made pizza crust (see note)
12 pieces Hormel turkey pepperoni
½ cup frozen corn, thawed
½ cup Sargento light grated four-cheese Mexican cheese

Preheat oven to 450 degrees F.

Spray baking sheet with nonstick cooking spray. Spread salsa evenly over pizza crust. Add turkey pepperoni and sprinkle on corn. Sprinkle cheese evenly on top. Place pizza on baking sheet and bake for 9 to 12 minutes.

Each serving provides:

328	Calories	3.2 g	Fiber
10.2 g	Fat	1147 mg	Sodium
18.1 g	Protein	24 mg	Cholesterol
43.2 g	Carbohydrates		

Diabetic exchanges: Lean meat, 3; starch, 2

Note: The lowfat, ready-made pizza crust can be found in the refrigerated section at the supermarket.

Green Chili–Cheese Pizza

⅓ cup mild salsa
1 (7-inch) Mama Mary pizza crust or other lowfat ready-
   made pizza crust (see note)
3 tablespoons chopped canned green chilies
¼ teaspoon garlic powder
¼ teaspoon onion powder
   Black pepper
½ cup Sargento light grated four-cheese Mexican cheese

Note: The lowfat ready-made pizza crust can be found in the refrigerated section at the supermarket.

Preheat oven to 450 degrees F.

Spray baking sheet with nonstick cooking spray. Spread salsa over surface of pizza crust. Top with green chilies and then sprinkle on garlic powder, onion powder, and black pepper to taste. Sprinkle cheese on top. Place pizza on baking sheet and bake for 7 to 10 minutes.

Each serving provides:

289	Calories	2.9 g	Fiber
8.7 g	Fat	967 mg	Sodium
14.6 g	Protein	10 mg	Cholesterol
40.3 g	Carbohydrates		

Diabetic exchanges: Lean meat, 2; vegetable, ½; starch, 2

SOUTHWEST GARLIC PIZZA (FOR GARLIC LOVERS)

SERVES 2

⅓ cup mild salsa

1 (7-inch) Mama Mary's pizza crust or other lowfat ready-made pizza crust (see note)

10 cloves garlic, each cut in half

¼ teaspoon fajita seasoning (approximately)

½ cup Sargento light grated four-cheese Mexican cheese

Preheat oven to 450 degrees F.

Spray baking sheet with nonstick cooking spray. Spread salsa over surface of pizza crust. Place garlic cloves evenly over pizza. Add fajita seasoning and sprinkle on cheese. Place pizza on baking sheet and bake for 7 to 10 minutes.

Each serving provides:

305	Calories	3 g	Fiber
8.8 g	Fat	1010 mg	Sodium
15.4 g	Protein	10 mg	Cholesterol
44.4 g	Carbohydrates		

Diabetic exchanges: Lean meat, 2; vegetable, 1½; starch, 2

Note: The lowfat ready-made pizza crust can be found in the refrigerated section at the supermarket.

Southwest Burgers

½ pound ground turkey breast
¼ cup onion, chopped
2 tablespoons chopped canned green chilies
1 clove garlic, pressed
¼ teaspoon chili powder
¼ teaspoon Tabasco sauce
   Salt and black pepper

Combine all ingredients in large bowl and mix thoroughly. Shape into 3 patties. Cook in large skillet sprayed with non-stick cooking spray over medium heat for 4 to 6 minutes or until desired doneness.

Serve on lowfat hamburger buns.

Each serving provides:

114	Calories	0.4 g	Fiber
4.2 g	Fat	43 mg	Sodium
16.4 g	Protein	41 mg	Cholesterol
1.8 g	Carbohydrates		

Diabetic exchange: Lean meat, 2

Chicken Taco Casserole

Serves 2

2 boneless, skinless chicken breasts (3 ounces each), cut into small pieces
1 tablespoon taco seasoning
¼ cup water
1 cup chopped canned tomatoes
1 small onion, chopped
¼ teaspoon garlic powder
¼ teaspoon onion powder
4 corn tortillas
¼ cup Sargento light grated Cheddar cheese
4 tablespoons fat-free sour cream

Preheat oven to 350 degrees F.

Spray medium skillet with nonstick cooking spray. Add chicken pieces and brown over medium heat. Add taco seasoning, water, tomatoes, and onion and stir. Simmer over low heat for 10 to 15 minutes. Add garlic powder and onion powder.

Spray glass loaf pan or small baking dish with nonstick cooking spray. Tear corn tortillas into large pieces. Layer pieces of tortilla, chicken mixture, cheese, and sour cream in dish. Bake for 25 to 30 minutes.

Each serving provides:

276	Calories	4.5 g	Fiber
4.5 g	Fat	746 mg	Sodium
29.5 g	Protein	54 mg	Cholesterol
30 g	Carbohydrates		

Diabetic exchanges: Lean meat, 2; starch, 2

Taco Meat Loaf

1 pound ground turkey breast
1 package (1¼ ounces) taco seasoning
½ large onion, chopped
½ teaspoon chili powder
1 fresh green chili pepper, seeded and chopped
1 cup tomato juice
1 egg white
1 clove garlic, pressed
3 corn tortillas, cut into small pieces

Preheat oven to 350 degrees F.

In large bowl, combine all ingredients, including tortilla pieces, and mix well. Spray loaf pan with nonstick cooking spray. Place meat mixture in loaf pan. Bake for 1 hour and 15 minutes.

Serve topped with salsa and fat-free sour cream if desired. This is also great with a baked potato or mashed potatoes. I like it sliced cold for sandwiches.

Each serving provides:

175	Calories	1.4 g	Fiber
5.2 g	Fat	212 mg	Sodium
18.4 g	Protein	41 mg	Cholesterol
13.1 g	Carbohydrates		

Diabetic exchanges: Lean meat, 2; vegetable, 1; starch, ½

Taos Omelet

Serves 2

1   cup fat-free liquid egg product
2   green onions, chopped
2   cloves garlic, pressed, or ¼ teaspoon garlic powder
2   tablespoons chopped canned green chilies
1   corn tortilla, cut or torn into small pieces
2   teaspoons Molly McButter butter sprinkles
    Salt and black pepper
    Chili powder (optional)
1   slice Kraft fat-free Cheddar cheese
3   tablespoons salsa
2   to 3 tablespoons fat-free sour cream

In medium bowl, combine egg product, green onions, garlic, chilies, corn tortilla pieces, butter sprinkles, salt and pepper to taste, and chili powder to taste if desired. Stir to mix.

Spray small skillet with nonstick cooking spray. Pour omelet mixture into skillet and cook over medium heat. As eggs start to cook and set, use a spatula and gently lift edges to allow uncooked egg to flow underneath. When omelet is set and fully cooked, place cheese slice on one half and fold omelet in half. Transfer to plate. Garnish with salsa and sour cream.

Each serving provides:

153	Calories	1.3 g	Fiber
1 g	Fat	681 mg	Sodium
18.3 g	Protein	2 mg	Cholesterol
17.2 g	Carbohydrates		

Diabetic exchanges: Lean meat, 1½; vegetable, 1; starch, ½

Spicy Tex-Mex Corn Pie

1	(9-inch) frozen Pet Ritz pie crust
½	cup fat-free sour cream
⅓	cup fat-free liquid egg product
1	can (15¼ ounces) corn, drained
1	green onion, chopped
1½	tablespoons chopped canned green chilies
1	tablespoon seeded and finely chopped green bell pepper
⅛	teaspoon garlic powder
½	tablespoon Tabasco jalapeño sauce (green)
½	teaspoon chili powder
	Salt and black pepper
1½	soft corn tortillas, cut into small pieces

Preheat oven to 350 degrees F.

Spray a 9-inch glass pie plate with nonstick cooking spray. Take the pie crust out of the foil baking pan and place it on the pie plate. Transferring the crust is easier if the crust is frozen. Shape the crust more to the pie plate after it has thawed.

In large bowl, combine sour cream and egg product. Stir until smooth. Add corn, green onion, chilies, bell pepper, garlic powder, Tabasco, chili powder, and salt and pepper to taste. Mix thoroughly. Add half the tortilla pieces (reserve the other half for topping).

Pour corn mixture into pie crust and top with remaining tortilla pieces. Bake for 35 to 40 minutes. Remove and serve warm. Garnish with sour cream and salsa if desired.

Each serving provides:

191	Calories	1.2 g	Fiber
6.3 g	Fat	301 mg	Sodium
5.9 g	Protein	4 mg	Cholesterol
27.9 g	Carbohydrates		

Diabetic exchanges: Lean meat, ½; vegetable, 2; starch, 1½

Hot and Spicy Meat Loaf

¾ pound ground turkey breast or chicken breast
2½ tablespoons fat-free liquid egg product
½ small green bell pepper, seeded and chopped
½ large onion, chopped
¼ teaspoon Worcestershire sauce
¼ teaspoon soy sauce
¼ teaspoon garlic powder
1½ stalks celery, chopped
¼ teaspoon black pepper
2½ tablespoons Tabasco jalapeño sauce (green)
¼ cup fat-free cracker crumbs
  Salt
  Sliced jalapeño peppers (optional)

Preheat oven to 350 degrees F.

In large bowl, combine all ingredients and mix well. Spray loaf pan with nonstick cooking spray. Place meat mixture in pan and bake for 1 hour. This is great with mashed potatoes or chilled and sliced for sandwiches.

Each serving provides:

131	Calories	0.8 g	Fiber
3.8 g	Fat	486 mg	Sodium
16.1 g	Protein	37 mg	Cholesterol
7.8 g	Carbohydrates		

Diabetic exchanges: Lean meat, 1½; starch, ½

Taos Casserole

½ pound ground turkey breast or chicken breast
½ teaspoon chili seasoning
1 can (14½ ounces) stewed tomatoes, chopped, with liquid
1 clove garlic, pressed
1 medium onion, chopped
  Salt and black pepper
½ cup fat-free sour cream
⅓ cup fat-free chicken broth
6 small corn tortillas
3 tablespoons chopped canned green chilies
½ cup fat-free liquid egg product
½ cup green chili enchilada sauce
½ cup Sargento light grated Cheddar cheese
¼ cup crushed baked tortilla chips

Preheat oven to 350 degrees F.

Spray large skillet with nonstick cooking spray. Add ground turkey or chicken and brown over medium heat. Add chili seasoning and tomatoes and simmer for 2 to 3 minutes. Add garlic and one-fourth of the chopped onion and simmer over low heat for about 10 minutes. Add salt and pepper to taste.

In small bowl, combine sour cream and chicken broth.

Spray a 7 × 11-inch casserole dish with nonstick cooking spray. Line bottom of casserole with 3 tortillas. Add a layer of green chilies and the remaining chopped onions. Add meat mixture. Top with egg product and another layer of the remaining 3 tortillas. Top with enchilada sauce and then the cheese. Pour sour cream mixture on top. Bake for 45 minutes. Add crushed tortilla chips the last 10 to 15 minutes of baking.

Each serving provides:

261	Calories	3.3 g	Fiber
5 g	Fat	659 mg	Sodium
19.2 g	Protein	26 mg	Cholesterol
35.3 g	Carbohydrates		

Diabetic exchanges: Lean meat, 2; starch, 2

ROASTED ROTEL CHICKEN BREASTS

SERVES 2

2 boneless, skinless chicken breasts (3 ounces each)
¼ cup all-purpose flour
  Salt and black pepper (optional)
½ cup canned Rotel tomatoes
½ small onion, chopped
⅛ teaspoon garlic powder
¼ cup fat-free chicken broth

Preheat oven to 350 degrees F.

Dip each chicken breast in flour on both sides. Spray medium skillet with nonstick cooking spray. Place chicken breasts in skillet. Season chicken breasts with salt and pepper to taste, if desired, and brown on both sides over medium heat.

In small bowl, combine tomatoes, onion, garlic powder, and chicken broth. Stir.

Spray 8-inch or 9-inch baking dish with nonstick cooking spray. Place chicken in dish. Cover with tomato mixture. Bake uncovered for 40 to 45 minutes. This is delicious served with rice or pasta.

Each serving provides:

220	Calories	1 g	Fiber
3.3 g	Fat	374 mg	Sodium
29.2 g	Protein	73 mg	Cholesterol
16.1 g	Carbohydrates		

Diabetic exchanges: Lean meat, 3; vegetable, 1; starch, 1

CHICKEN WITH TOMATILLO SALSA

SERVES 2

2 boneless, skinless chicken breasts (3 ounces each)
¼ cup all-purpose flour
¼ cup fat-free chicken broth
½ medium onion, chopped
⅓ cup (11½ ounces) Guiltless Gourmet green
   tomatillo salsa
   Black pepper

Preheat oven to 350 degrees F.

Spray large skillet with nonstick cooking spray. Dip each
chicken breast in flour on both sides and place in skillet.
Cook over medium heat until golden brown. Spray baking

dish with nonstick cooking spray. Place chicken in dish. Pour chicken broth over chicken. Sprinkle onion on top of each piece of chicken and then spoon salsa on top. Add black pepper to taste. Bake for 35 to 40 minutes.

For a delicious variation, replace the green tomatillo salsa with an equal amount of Guiltless Gourmet roasted red pepper salsa.

Each serving provides:

242	Calories	2.3 g	Fiber
4 g	Fat	578 mg	Sodium
29.7 g	Protein	73 mg	Cholesterol
20.5 g	Carbohydrates		

Diabetic exchanges: Lean meat, 3; starch, 1

SANTA FE OMELET

SERVES 1

2 tablespoons Tostitos salsa con queso (cheese dip)
⅓ cup fat-free sour cream
5 egg whites
1 tablespoon Molly McButter butter sprinkles
2 green onions, chopped
1 fresh green chili pepper, seeded and chopped,
   or 2 teaspoons chopped canned green chilies
¼ cup cooked boneless, skinless chicken breast cut into
   small pieces

In small bowl, stir together cheese dip and sour cream. Mix thoroughly and set aside.

In medium bowl, lightly whisk together egg whites and butter sprinkles. Add onions and chili pepper or chilies and mix. Add chicken pieces and whisk slightly.

Spray small skillet with nonstick cooking spray. Pour egg white mixture into skillet and cook over medium heat. Do not stir. As edges of omelet start to cook, use a spatula and lift edges to allow uncooked liquid to flow underneath. Repeat this process a couple of times. Cover and simmer for a minute or two until all of the egg is cooked. Remove omelet to a plate and fold in half.

Warm the cheese sauce in the microwave for 25 to 30 seconds. When sauce is warm, pour over omelet and serve. Garnish with salsa if desired.

Each serving provides:

280	Calories	2 g	Fiber
3.7 g	Fat	1547 mg	Sodium
35.8 g	Protein	34 mg	Cholesterol
23.7 g	Carbohydrates		

Diabetic exchanges: Lean meat, 3; vegetable, 1; starch, 1

Chicken Chimichangas

2   boneless, skinless chicken breasts (3 ounces each),
    cut into strips
2   teaspoons taco seasoning
½   small onion, chopped
½   clove garlic, pressed
¼   cup red enchilada sauce
2   large fat-free flour tortillas
½   can (4 ounces) whole green chilies, cut into long strips
2   tablespoons Tostitos salsa con queso (cheese dip)
2   tablespoons fat-free sour cream

Spray large skillet with nonstick cooking spray. Place chicken strips in skillet and brown on one side over medium heat. Turn chicken and sprinkle taco seasoning over it. Add onion, garlic, and enchilada sauce and simmer over low heat until sauce around chicken is very thick.

Warm tortillas (a simple way to do this is to microwave them on high for 10 to 15 seconds). Place each tortilla flat on a plate and place a few strips of chicken on top, about an inch from one edge. Include a little sauce with the chicken strips. Add about 2 strips of green chilies, fold edge of tortilla over chicken, and roll. About halfway through rolling, fold edges inside and then finish rolling. After tortillas are rolled, place on a microwave-safe serving plate and drizzle 1 tablespoon cheese dip on each chimichanga and top with 1 tablespoon sour cream. Cook in microwave on high for 15 to 20 seconds and serve.

Each serving provides:

287	Calories	12.1 g	Fiber
3.5 g	Fat	1492 mg	Sodium
26.3 g	Protein	51 mg	Cholesterol
37.6 g	Carbohydrates		

Diabetic exchanges: Lean meat, 3; vegetable, 1; starch, ½

BLACKENED CHICKEN ENCHILADAS

SERVES 4

2 boneless, skinless chicken breasts, cut into strips
   Garlic salt or powder
   Any blackened spice (see note)
1 medium onion, sliced
4 fat-free fajita-size flour tortillas
¾ cup fat-free sour cream
4 tablespoons Tostitos salsa con queso (cheese dip)
6 tablespoons fat-free chicken broth
½ tablespoon Molly McButter butter sprinkles

Preheat oven to 350 degrees F.

Spray a large skillet with nonstick cooking spray. Place chicken strips in skillet and season with garlic salt or powder and blackened spices to taste. Season lightly for a mild taste and heavy for a spicy, hot taste. Cook over medium heat for 3 to 4 minutes, until chicken is browned and tender.

Note: I recommend Chef Paul Prudhomme's Blackened Chicken Magic.

Spray another medium skillet with nonstick cooking spray and simmer onion over medium heat. Keep covered and turn occasionally. Cook until lightly brown and tender.

Spray a small casserole dish with nonstick cooking spray. Place 2 to 3 strips of chicken in the center of each tortilla. Add several pieces of onion, roll up, and place in casserole dish.

In food processor, combine sour cream, cheese dip, chicken broth, and butter sprinkles and blend. Pour sauce over tortillas and bake for 30 to 35 minutes.

Each serving provides:

242	Calories	10.8 g	Fiber
2.9 g	Fat	789 mg	Sodium
18.7 g	Protein	31 mg	Cholesterol
35.2 g	Carbohydrates		

Diabetic exchanges: Lean meat, 2; starch, 1⅔

Two-Way Chili

½ pound ground turkey breast

2 teaspoons William's chili seasoning

1 can (14½ ounces) stewed tomatoes, chopped, with liquid

½ cup fat-free chicken broth

½ teaspoon garlic powder

½ medium onion, chopped

1 can (15 ounces) chili beans (do not drain)

1 to 2 cups water

⅛ teaspoon onion powder

1 teaspoon sugar

½ cup uncooked macaroni

Spray large saucepan with nonstick cooking spray. Add ground turkey and brown over medium heat. Add chili seasoning and stir. Add tomatoes, chicken broth, garlic powder, onion, chili beans, water, onion powder, and sugar.

Simmer over medium-low heat for 45 minutes. Add macaroni and cook an additional 15 to 20 minutes. Serve with a dollop of sour cream on top, if desired. I also like it topped with crumbled baked tortilla chips.

Each serving provides:

200	Calories	4.4 g	Fiber
0.9 g	Fat	686 mg	Sodium
15.1 g	Protein	23 mg	Cholesterol
33.6 g	Carbohydrates		

Diabetic exchanges: Lean meat, ¾; starch, 2

Vegetable-Stuffed Enchiladas

½	carrot, sliced
¼	cup fat-free chicken broth
¾	cup fresh mushrooms, sliced
½	small zucchini, sliced
½	small yellow squash, sliced
½	medium onion, sliced
1	fresh green chili pepper, seeded and sliced
½	tablespoon chopped fresh cilantro
2	teaspoons taco seasoning
¼	teaspoon garlic salt
½	clove garlic, pressed
½	medium tomato, chopped
3	small fat-free flour tortillas
2½	tablespoons evaporated skim milk
¼	cup Sargento light grated Cheddar cheese
1	green onion (including white part), chopped
¼	teaspoon garlic salt

Preheat oven to 350 degrees F.

Spray large skillet with nonstick cooking spray. Add carrot and 2 tablespoons chicken broth. Simmer over medium heat and stir for 2 to 3 minutes. Add mushrooms and simmer for 2 to 3 minutes. Add zucchini, squash, onion, chili pepper, cilantro, taco seasoning, garlic salt, and garlic. Add remaining chicken broth. Simmer over medium heat and stir for 2 to 3 minutes, until vegetables are partially done. Add tomato. *Do not overcook*—leave some crunch in vegetables. Remove from heat and cool slightly.

Place about ¼ cup of the mixture on each tortilla and roll; arrange in baking dish sprayed with nonstick cooking spray.

In a medium bowl, combine milk, cheese, green onion, and garlic salt. Pour over enchiladas. Bake for 25 to 30 minutes. Garnish with salsa or fat-free sour cream if desired.

Each serving provides:

138	Calories	7.2 g	Fiber
2.3 g	Fat	1007 mg	Sodium
7.9 g	Protein	4 mg	Cholesterol
23.7 g	Carbohydrates		

Diabetic exchanges: Lean meat, 1; starch, 1

TOSTADAS

SERVES 3

3   small corn tortillas
    Garlic salt
½   cup fat-free refried beans
¼   cup fat-free sour cream
½   medium onion, chopped
½   cup Sargento light grated Cheddar cheese
½   large tomato, chopped
1½ cups chopped lettuce

Preheat oven to 375 degrees F.

Spray cookie sheet with Buttermist or other butter-flavored nonstick cooking spray. Place tortillas on cookie sheet. Lightly spray tops of tortillas with nonstick cooking spray and season with garlic salt to taste. Place another cookie sheet on top of tortillas so they will bake flat and not curl. Bake for 10 to 12 minutes. Remove and cool slightly.

Spread each tortilla with refried beans and sour cream. Top with onion, cheese, tomato, and lettuce. (Divide all topping ingredients into thirds and distribute evenly.)

Each serving provides:

184	Calories	4.8 g	Fiber
3.8 g	Fat	393 mg	Sodium
11.2 g	Protein	7 mg	Cholesterol
28.7 g	Carbohydrates		

Diabetic exchanges: Lean meat, 1; vegetable, 2; starch, 1

Spicy Chicken with Creamy Jalapeño Sauce

Serves 2

2	boneless, skinless chicken breasts (3 ounces each)
	Garlic powder
	Onion powder
	Chili powder
¾	cup fat-free chicken broth
¼	cup Campbell's condensed cheese soup
2	teaspoons Tabasco jalapeño sauce (green)
1½	tablespoons cornstarch
2	tablespoons fat-free sour cream

Spray small skillet with nonstick cooking spray. Season chicken breasts with garlic powder, onion powder, and chili powder to taste. Brown and cook over low heat until done, 15 to 20 minutes, turning chicken as necessary.

In small saucepan, combine chicken broth, cheese soup, jalapeño sauce, cornstarch, and sour cream. Stir over medium heat until sauce thickens. Pour sauce over chicken breasts.

Each serving provides:

169	Calories	0.1 g	Fiber
3.6 g	Fat	748 mg	Sodium
22.5 g	Protein	55 mg	Cholesterol
10.5 g	Carbohydrates		

Diabetic exchanges: Lean meat, 3; starch, ⅔

WHITE CHILI, SOUTHWEST STYLE

SERVES 4

1 cup dry white beans
1 can (14½ ounces) fat-free chicken broth
1 cup water
1 boneless, skinless chicken breast (3 ounces),
   cut into small pieces
½ medium onion, chopped
½ stalk celery, chopped
2 tablespoons chopped canned green chilies
1 clove garlic, pressed
1 teaspoon chili powder
   Salt and black pepper
¼ cup fat-free sour cream

Rinse and sort beans, then cover with water in medium pot. Bring to boil; remove from heat and let stand 1 hour. Drain. Add chicken broth and water and simmer over medium heat.

Spray medium skillet with nonstick cooking spray. Add chicken, onion, and celery and brown over medium heat.

Add chicken mixture to beans along with chilies, garlic, chili powder, and salt and pepper to taste. Simmer over low heat for 2 to 3 hours or until beans are done. Add sour cream and stir into the chili just before serving.

Each serving provides:

236	Calories	9 g	Fiber
0.9 g	Fat	499 mg	Sodium
20.2 g	Protein	12 mg	Cholesterol
38.1 g	Carbohydrates		

Diabetic exchanges: Lean meat, 2; starch, 1½

Veggie Fajitas

Serves 3

1   teaspoon sesame seeds
½   large onion, sliced
½   bell pepper, seeded and sliced
½   small zucchini, sliced
½   small yellow squash, sliced
1½   fresh green chilies, seeded and sliced lengthwise
½   cup fresh mushrooms, sliced
1   teaspoon fajita seasoning
½   teaspoon garlic salt
     Black pepper
¼   cup Sargento light grated Cheddar cheese
3   small flour tortillas

Spray large skillet with nonstick cooking spray. Add sesame seeds and lightly brown seeds over low heat for about 1 minute. Add onion and brown. Add bell pepper, zucchini, squash, chilies, mushrooms, fajita seasoning, garlic salt, and black pepper to taste. Stir over medium heat just until vegetables are tender, 2 to 3 minutes. *Do not overcook!* Stir in cheese just before serving. Spoon mixture on tortillas and roll. Garnish with salsa if desired, and serve.

Each serving provides:

133	Calories	3.6 g	Fiber
2.8 g	Fat	524 mg	Sodium
6 g	Protein	3 mg	Cholesterol
22.1 g	Carbohydrates		

Diabetic exchanges: Lean meat, ½; vegetable, 1; starch, 1

Taco Casserole

1 small onion, chopped
½ cup fat-free refried beans
½ pound ground turkey breast
2 teaspoons taco seasoning
¼ cup water
⅓ cup Campbell's 98 percent fat-free condensed cream of mushroom soup
2 tablespoons chopped canned green chilies
¼ cup fat-free sour cream
¼ cup Sargento light grated Cheddar cheese
½ cup crushed baked tortilla chips

Preheat oven to 350 degrees F.

In a bowl, combine half of the chopped onion with the refried beans. Spray a 9 × 13-inch casserole with nonstick cooking spray and line the bottom with the mixture.

Spray medium skillet with nonstick cooking spray. Add ground turkey and brown over medium heat. Add taco seasoning and stir. Add water and stir. Add cream of mushroom soup and chilies and remove from heat. Add sour cream and mix thoroughly.

Pour mixture over refried bean mixture in casserole. Add remaining onion. Sprinkle cheese on top, then crushed tortilla chips. Bake for 25 to 35 minutes.

Each serving provides:

195	Calories	4.1 g	Fiber
2.4 g	Fat	629 mg	Sodium
17.6 g	Protein	30 mg	Cholesterol
27.1 g	Carbohydrates		

Diabetic exchanges: Lean meat, 2; starch, 1

Tasty Bacon
and Egg Burrito

½ teaspoon dry onion flakes
½ cup fat-free liquid egg product
1 slice turkey bacon, cooked and crumbled
¼ cup Sargento light grated Cheddar cheese
1 tablespoon chopped canned green chilies
  Salt and black pepper
  Dash of Tabasco sauce (optional)
1 tablespoon fat-free sour cream
1 small fat-free flour tortilla

In small bowl, combine onion flakes and egg product. Set aside for 5 to 10 minutes, to let onion flakes soften.

In another small bowl, combine egg mixture with bacon, cheese, chilies, salt and pepper to taste, and Tabasco and mix. Spray medium skillet with nonstick cooking spray. Add

MAIN DISHES

144

mixture and scramble over medium-low heat. Cheese will burn if heat is too high.

When egg mixture is almost done, stir in sour cream. Place on tortilla and roll up. Enjoy.

Each serving provides:

219	Calories	4.4 g	Fiber
6.2 g	Fat	714 mg	Sodium
25.2 g	Protein	20 mg	Cholesterol
16.4 g	Carbohydrates		

Diabetic exchanges: Lean meat, 2½; starch, 1

GREEN CHILI ENCHILADAS

SERVES 3

1   small onion, sliced fairly thin
1½   teaspoons taco seasoning
1   can (4 ounces) whole green chilies, drained
3   soft corn tortillas
6   tablespoons Sargento light grated Cheddar cheese
½   cup green chili enchilada sauce

Preheat oven to 350 degrees F.

Spray medium skillet with nonstick cooking spray. Add onion and brown over medium heat. Sprinkle 1 teaspoon taco seasoning on onion. Add a little water if onion gets too dry while browning.

Slice open each green chili and spread flat. Warm tortillas in microwave according to package directions. Place chilies on each tortilla. Sprinkle about 2 tablespoons cheese on top of chilies. Add some onion and roll up each tortilla. Spray small baking dish with nonstick cooking spray. Place enchiladas close together in baking dish. Pour enchilada sauce over the top. Sprinkle remaining ½ teaspoon taco seasoning over sauce and bake for 30 to 35 minutes.

Each serving provides:

146	Calories	2.9 g	Fiber
4 g	Fat	514 mg	Sodium
6.4 g	Protein	5 mg	Cholesterol
21.9 g	Carbohydrates		

Diabetic exchanges: Lean meat, ½; vegetable, 1; starch, 1

ENCHILADA CASSEROLE

⅓ pound ground turkey breast or chicken breast
2 teaspoons enchilada seasoning
3 soft corn tortillas
3 tablespoons fat-free sour cream
¼ cup fat-free chicken broth
¾ cup canned corn, drained
1 can (4 ounces) chopped green chilies
½ cup chopped onion
⅓ cup green chili enchilada sauce
¾ cup Sargento light grated Cheddar cheese

Preheat oven to 350 degrees F.

Spray skillet with nonstick cooking spray. Add ground turkey and brown over medium heat. Sprinkle enchilada seasoning on the meat and stir. Set aside.

Spray 8-inch casserole dish with nonstick cooking spray. Line bottom and sides of dish with tortillas. In a bowl, combine sour cream with chicken broth and set aside.

Place the corn on top of the tortillas to make the first layer, then layer the chilies, then the onion, and then the meat. Pour the sour cream mixture over the casserole and then pour in the enchilada sauce. Top casserole with cheese and bake for 40 to 45 minutes.

Each serving provides:

219	Calories	2.4 g	Fiber
5.2 g	Fat	692 mg	Sodium
18.5 g	Protein	30 mg	Cholesterol
25.4 g	Carbohydrates		

Diabetic exchanges: Lean meat, 2; starch, 1½

Hot and Spicy Southwest Shrimp

½ cup chopped onion
2 carrots, sliced
9 large shrimp, cooked
½ fresh jalapeño pepper, seeded and sliced
1 cup spicy tomato juice
1 clove garlic, pressed
¼ teaspoon chili powder
⅛ teaspoon ground cumin
⅛ teaspoon dried oregano
¼ teaspoon salt
Juice of ½ lime
Dash of seasoned salt
Dash of Tabasco sauce
Black pepper

Spray skillet with nonstick cooking spray. Add onion and brown over medium heat. Cook carrots in microwave for 2 to 3 minutes, until slightly tender. Do not overcook. Add shrimp to onion. Add carrots, jalapeño pepper, tomato juice, garlic, chili powder, cumin, oregano, salt, lime juice, seasoned salt, Tabasco, and pepper to taste. Simmer over very low heat for 8 to 10 minutes. This is great served over rice.

Each serving provides:

143	Calories	1.8 g	Fiber
1.3 g	Fat	715 mg	Sodium
20.8 g	Protein	178 mg	Cholesterol
12.5 g	Carbohydrates		

Diabetic exchanges: Lean meat, 2; vegetable, 1½

Mexican Quiche

1 cup fat-free liquid egg product
¼ cup 1 percent cottage cheese
3 tablespoons fat-free sour cream
2 tablespoons all-purpose flour
½ cup Sargento light grated Cheddar cheese
2 tablespoons chopped canned green chilies
⅛ cup chopped onion

Preheat oven to 350 degrees.

In food processor or blender, combine egg product, cottage cheese, sour cream, and flour. Process until no lumps remain. Pour into large bowl. Add cheese, chilies, and onion and stir. Spray 9-inch pie plate with nonstick cooking spray. Pour mixture into pie plate. Bake for 40 to 45 minutes.

Each serving provides:

67	Calories	0.2 g	Fiber
1.6 g	Fat	180 mg	Sodium
8.6 g	Protein	4 mg	Cholesterol
4.5 g	Carbohydrates		

Diabetic exchanges: Lean meat, 1; vegetable, ½

Tasty Taco Meat

SERVES 3

½ pound ground turkey breast or chicken breast
1 small onion, chopped
¼ cup thick-and-chunky salsa
1 teaspoon taco seasoning

Spray skillet with nonstick cooking spray. Add ground turkey and brown over medium heat. Add onion and brown 5 to 6 minutes longer. Add salsa and mix well. Add taco seasoning and cook to desired consistency.

Serve hot, rolled in flour or corn tortilla, or chill the mixture and serve cold on top of tossed salad for a taco salad. If filling a tortilla, add chopped lettuce and tomato and ½ tablespoon fat-free sour cream to each tortilla.

Each serving provides:

118	Calories	1.6 g	Fiber
1.5 g	Fat	635 mg	Sodium
19 g	Protein	46 mg	Cholesterol
6.4 g	Carbohydrates		

Diabetic exchanges: Lean meat, 2

CHEESY CHICKEN ENCHILADAS

SERVES 4

2   boneless, skinless chicken breasts (3 ounces each), cut into long strips
1   cup chopped white onion
2   tablespoons fat-free sour cream
⅛   cup fat-free mayonnaise
1   tablespoon fat-free chicken broth
1¼ cups Sargento light grated Cheddar cheese
½   cup green chili enchilada sauce
4   soft corn tortillas

Preheat oven to 375 degrees F.

Spray medium skillet with nonstick cooking spray. Add chicken and brown over medium heat. When the chicken breasts are golden brown, add onion and cook for 5 to 7 minutes or until onions are browned also. Remove from heat and set aside.

In small mixing bowl, combine sour cream and mayonnaise. Very gradually add chicken broth, stirring constantly. Do not add broth too fast, or mixture will be lumpy. When thoroughly mixed, pour into small saucepan and cook over medium heat, stirring constantly, until mixture starts to boil. Add 1 cup of the cheese and stir over low heat until cheese is melted. Set aside.

Pour enchilada sauce into large shallow bowl. Dip each tortilla in the sauce and make sure both sides are covered. Fill each tortilla with chicken, onion, and a little cheese. (Save ¼ cup cheese for topping.) Roll up each tortilla and place in small casserole dish sprayed with nonstick cooking spray. Pour sour cream mixture over enchiladas. Sprinkle remaining cheese on top. Cover and bake for 20 to 25 minutes. Garnish with salsa if desired.

Each serving provides:

225	Calories	2.3 g	Fiber
6.2 g	Fat	738 mg	Sodium
21 g	Protein	34 mg	Cholesterol
21.7 g	Carbohydrates		

Diabetic exchanges: Lean meat, 2; vegetable, 1½; starch, 1

ZESTY CHICKEN FAJITAS

SERVES 3

1½ large green bell peppers, seeded and cut into
     long strips
1½ large white onions, sliced
½   package fajita seasoning
2   boneless, skinless chicken breasts (3 ounces each),
     cut into long strips
3   small soft fat-free flour tortillas
     Light grated cheddar cheese, salsa, chopped tomato,
     lettuce, or fat-free sour cream for garnish (optional)

Spray a large skillet with nonstick cooking spray. Brown and
simmer bell peppers and onions over low heat, stirring fre-
quently, 15 to 20 minutes. Sprinkle half the fajita seasoning
on the peppers and onions. Be sure to cover with a lid. Add
about ¼ cup water if the skillet becomes dry.

The chicken has a better flavor if cooked on a charcoal grill, but it may be cooked in a skillet or in the broiler. Place chicken pieces on grill and sprinkle with remaining fajita seasoning. Cook 1½ minutes on each side. *Do not overcook!* Serve chicken strips rolled in flour tortillas along with peppers and onions and any of the desired listed toppings for garnish.

Each serving provides:

192	Calories	6.4 g	Fiber
2.5 g	Fat	280 mg	Sodium
20.8 g	Protein	49 mg	Cholesterol
20.8 g	Carbohydrates		

Diabetic exchanges: Lean meat, 2; starch, 1

Fiesta Meat and Bean Burrito

½   pound ground turkey breast or chicken breast
1   tablespoon dry onion flakes
2   tablespoons chopped canned green chilies
1½ tablespoons salsa
    Salt and black pepper
¾   cup canned fat-free refried beans
4   fat-free flour tortillas

Spray large skillet with nonstick cooking spray. Add ground turkey and brown over medium heat. Add onion flakes, chilies, and salsa to meat as it is cooking. Add salt and pepper to taste. Remove from heat, add refried beans, and stir together.

Warm tortillas in microwave for 7 to 10 seconds. Wrap meat and bean mixture in tortillas.

Each serving provides:

169	Calories	7.1 g	Fiber
1.2 g	Fat	411 mg	Sodium
18 g	Protein	34 mg	Cholesterol
23 g	Carbohydrates		

Diabetic exchanges: Lean meat, 1½; starch, 1

Tex-Mex–Style Chili

⅓ pound ground turkey breast or chicken breast
½ cup tomato sauce
1 cup chopped stewed tomatoes
2 teaspoons chili seasoning
1 cup water
½ small onion, chopped
⅛ teaspoon garlic powder
½ cup canned black beans or pinto beans (optional)
  Salt

Spray skillet with nonstick cooking spray. Add ground turkey and brown over medium heat. Add tomato sauce, tomatoes, chili seasoning, water, onion, garlic powder, beans if desired, and salt to taste. Simmer over low heat until desired thickness is reached.

Each serving provides:

222	Calories	7.3 g	Fiber
2.2 g	Fat	1138 mg	Sodium
23.7 g	Protein	45 mg	Cholesterol
28.2 g	Carbohydrates		

Diabetic exchanges: Lean meat, 2; starch, 1½

Mexican Beans

SERVES 4

1 cup dry pinto beans
1 can (14½ ounces) fat-free chicken broth
1 small onion, chopped
1 clove garlic, pressed
¼ teaspoon onion powder
½ cup canned salsa verde
  Juice of 1 lime
  Salt and black pepper

Rinse beans and soak overnight. Rinse again, cover with water, and cook over low heat for at least 2 hours (I prefer 3 hours). About halfway through cooking beans, add chicken broth, onion, garlic, onion powder, salsa verde, lime juice, and salt and pepper to taste and simmer for at least an hour.

Each serving provides:

342	Calories	20.6 g	Fiber
1.5 g	Fat	687 mg	Sodium
20.3 g	Protein	0 mg	Cholesterol
64 g	Carbohydrates		

Diabetic exchanges: Vegetable, 1; starch, 4

Garlic Chicken with Garlic Cheese Sauce

2   boneless, skinless chicken breasts (3 ounces each)
    Garlic powder
    Black pepper
¾   cup fat-free chicken broth
4   cloves garlic, pressed
1½ tablespoons cornstarch
2   tablespoons fat-free sour cream
¼   cup Campbell's condensed cheese soup
1   tablespoon dry onion flakes
    Dash of chili powder

Spray small skillet with nonstick cooking spray. Season chicken with garlic powder and pepper to taste. Brown and cook over low heat until done, 15 to 20 minutes.

In small saucepan, combine chicken broth, garlic, cornstarch, sour cream, cheese soup, onion flakes, and chili powder. Stir over medium heat until sauce thickens. Pour sauce over chicken breasts.

Each serving provides:

184	Calories	0.4 g	Fiber
3.6 g	Fat	661 mg	Sodium
23.1 g	Protein	55 mg	Cholesterol
14.4 g	Carbohydrates		

Diabetic exchanges: Lean meat, 2½; starch, ½

Sesame Chicken with Spicy Cheese Sauce

2   boneless, skinless chicken breasts (3 ounces each)
2   tablespoons sesame seeds
    Garlic powder
    Onion powder
    Black pepper
    Salt (optional)
¾   cup fat-free chicken broth
2   teaspoons chopped canned green chilies
¼   cup Campbell's condensed cheese soup
1½ tablespoons cornstarch
    Dash of garlic powder
2   tablespoons fat-free sour cream

Spray small skillet with nonstick cooking spray. Sprinkle chicken breasts with sesame seeds and season with garlic powder, onion powder, and pepper to taste; add salt to taste if desired. Brown and cook over low heat until done, 15 to 20 minutes.

In small saucepan, combine chicken broth, chilies, cheese soup, cornstarch, garlic powder, and sour cream. Stir over medium heat until sauce thickens. Pour sauce over chicken.

Each serving provides:

221	Calories	1.1 g	Fiber
8.1 g	Fat	670 mg	Sodium
24.1 g	Protein	55 mg	Cholesterol
12.6 g	Carbohydrates		

Diabetic exchanges: Lean meat, 3; starch, ⅔

QUICK CHILI PIE

SERVES 6

- ¾ cup cornmeal
- 1 can (14½ ounces) fat-free chicken broth
- ¼ teaspoon chili powder
  Dash of garlic salt
- 1 can (15 ounces) 99 percent fat-free turkey chili with beans
- 1 medium onion, chopped
- 1 clove garlic, pressed
- ¼ cup Sargento light grated Cheddar cheese

Preheat oven to 350 degrees F.

In small saucepan, combine cornmeal, chicken broth, chili powder, and garlic salt. Stir over medium heat until thick. Spray an 8-inch square baking dish with nonstick cooking spray. Pour cornmeal mixture into baking dish.

In medium bowl, combine chili, onion, and garlic. Very lightly add this mixture to the cornmeal mixture. Do not completely mix; the chili should sort of ribbon through the cornmeal. Sprinkle cheese on top and bake for 40 to 45 minutes.

Each serving provides:

161	Calories	2.7 g	Fiber
2.4 g	Fat	660 mg	Sodium
10.1 g	Protein	17 mg	Cholesterol
25.3 g	Carbohydrates		

Diabetic exchanges: Lean meat, 1; starch, 1½

TACO TAMALE PIE

SERVES 4

¾ cup cornmeal
¼ teaspoon chili powder
1 can (14½ ounces) fat-free chicken broth
⅓ pound extra-lean ground beef
1 small onion, chopped
2 cloves garlic, pressed
1 package (1¼ ounces) taco seasoning
½ cup water
1 cup frozen corn, thawed
   Salt and black pepper
¼ cup Sargento light grated Cheddar cheese

Preheat oven to 350 degrees F.

In medium saucepan, combine cornmeal, chili powder, and chicken broth. Stir over medium heat until very thick, 10 to 15 minutes. Spray an 8-inch-square baking dish with non-stick cooking spray. Press and pat crust mixture on bottom and sides of dish. Set aside.

Spray medium skillet with nonstick cooking spray. Add ground beef, onion, and garlic and brown over medium heat. Simmer about 10 minutes. Add taco seasoning and water. Stir and simmer about 2 minutes. Add corn and salt and pepper to taste. Pour this mixture into crust. Sprinkle cheese on top. Bake for 35 to 40 minutes.

Each serving provides:

186	Calories	2.6 g	Fiber
5.7 g	Fat	781 mg	Sodium
9.8 g	Protein	19 mg	Cholesterol
24.7 g	Carbohydrates		

Diabetic exchanges: Lean meat, 2; starch, 1

Veggie Tamale Pie

Serves 4

Crust

¾ cup cornmeal
½ teaspoon Molly McButter butter sprinkles
1 can (14½ ounces) fat-free chicken broth
¼ teaspoon chili powder
  Dash of garlic salt

Filling

1 cup frozen corn, thawed
1 cup white hominy
1 small onion, chopped
1 tablespoon seeded and finely chopped red bell pepper
2 cloves garlic, pressed
  Dash of garlic salt
  Black pepper
¼ cup Sargento light grated Cheddar cheese

Preheat oven to 350 degrees F.

In a saucepan, combine cornmeal, butter sprinkles, chicken broth, chili powder, and garlic salt. Cook over medium heat until thick, about 10 minutes. Spray an 8-inch-square baking dish with nonstick cooking spray. Press and pat crust mixture into bottom of dish. Save about ½ cup of crust mixture to dot on top.

In medium bowl, combine corn, hominy, onion, bell pepper, garlic, garlic salt, and pepper to taste, and stir. Pour this mixture into crust and dot with remaining crust mix. Sprinkle with cheese and bake for 35 to 40 minutes.

Each serving provides:

137	Calories	2.3 g	Fiber
1.2 g	Fat	470 mg	Sodium
5.1 g	Protein	2 mg	Cholesterol
27.3 g	Carbohydrates		

Diabetic exchanges: Lean meat, ½; vegetable, 1; starch, 1

Veggie Enchiladas

Serves 2

1½ cups mixed raw vegetables, such as broccoli, cauli-
flower, and bell peppers
1 small onion, sliced
½ cup fat-free chicken broth
Garlic salt
Black pepper
Chili powder
2 lowfat flour tortillas (each 8 inches in diameter)
4 tablespoons fat-free sour cream
4 teaspoons chopped fresh cilantro
½ cup green chili enchilada sauce
¼ cup Sargento light grated four-cheese Mexican cheese

Preheat oven to 350 degrees F.

Spray medium skillet with nonstick cooking spray. Add mixed raw vegetables and onion. Cook over medium-low heat and add chicken broth as needed for moisture. Eventually, pour in all of chicken broth and season vegetables with garlic salt, black pepper, and chili powder to taste. Simmer over low heat 4 to 6 minutes, until vegetables are done. Divide vegetables into two equal portions.

Place one half of vegetable mixture on each tortilla. To each tortilla, add 2 tablespoons sour cream and 2 teaspoons cilantro and roll up. Spray glass baking dish with nonstick cooking spray. Place enchiladas in baking dish. Pour enchilada sauce over the enchiladas and then sprinkle cheese on top. Bake for about 25 minutes.

Each serving provides:

244	Calories	5.4 g	Fiber
4.6 g	Fat	957 mg	Sodium
12.2 g	Protein	5 mg	Cholesterol
42 g	Carbohydrates		

Diabetic exchanges: Lean meat, ½; vegetable, 2; starch, 2

Green Chili Stew with Chicken

Serves 3

2 boneless, skinless chicken breasts (3 ounces each), cut into small pieces
1 can (14½ ounces) fat-free chicken broth
1 clove garlic, pressed
2 large carrots, sliced
1 small onion, chopped
1 can (4 ounces) whole green chilies, chopped
1 tablespoon chopped fresh cilantro
2 cups water
  Juice of 1 lime
  Salt and black pepper
  Dash of chili powder
3 tablespoons fat-free sour cream

Spray medium pot with nonstick cooking spray. Add chicken and brown over medium heat. Add chicken broth, garlic, carrots, onion, chilies, cilantro, water, lime juice, salt and pepper to taste, and chili powder. Simmer over very low heat for about 45 minutes or until carrots are done. Stir in fat-free sour cream and serve.

Each serving provides:

125	Calories	1.6 g	Fiber
0.9 g	Fat	711 mg	Sodium
16.8 g	Protein	33 mg	Cholesterol
12.4 g	Carbohydrates		

Diabetic exchanges: Lean meat, 1½; vegetable, 2

Cheesy Spinach Enchiladas

½   cup 1 percent cottage cheese
½   cup fresh spinach, torn into small pieces
1   clove garlic, pressed
4   green onions, chopped
¼   cup Sargento light grated Cheddar cheese
2   small lowfat flour tortillas
¾   cup fat-free chicken broth
2   tablespoons Old El Paso lowfat cheese and salsa dip
2   tablespoons fat-free sour cream
⅛   teaspoon garlic powder
1½ tablespoons cornstarch

Preheat oven to 350 degrees F.

In medium bowl, combine cottage cheese, spinach, garlic, green onions, and cheese. Roll half of mixture in each tortilla. Place in glass baking dish sprayed with nonstick cooking spray. Bake for 30 to 35 minutes.

Meanwhile, in small pan, combine chicken broth, cheese dip, sour cream, garlic powder, and cornstarch. Stir over medium heat until sauce thickens slightly. Pour sauce over enchiladas just before serving.

Each serving provides:

219	Calories	1.7 g	Fiber
3.9 g	Fat	1096 mg	Sodium
15.8 g	Protein	8 mg	Cholesterol
30.9 g	Carbohydrates		

Diabetic exchanges: Lean meat, 2; vegetable, 1; starch, 1

BAKED FAJITAS

2 boneless, skinless chicken breasts (3 ounces each),
   cut into strips
½ bell pepper, seeded and sliced
1 medium onion, sliced
   Garlic powder
   Black pepper
   Fajita seasoning
2 small fat-free flour tortillas
½ cup fat-free chicken broth
¼ cup fat-free sour cream
3 slices Kraft fat-free sharp Cheddar cheese, torn into
   small pieces
   Salt and black pepper

Preheat oven to 350 degrees F.

Spray large skillet with nonstick cooking spray. Add chicken and brown over medium heat. Add bell pepper and onion. Cover and simmer over low heat until onions are soft and cooked. Season with garlic powder, black pepper, and fajita seasoning to taste.

Roll chicken mixture in tortillas and place in small baking dish. Add 2 tablespoons of the chicken broth and bake for 20 minutes.

Meanwhile, in small saucepan, combine remaining chicken broth, sour cream, cheese, and salt and pepper to taste. Stir over medium heat until cheese melts. Pour sauce over fajitas and serve.

Each serving provides:

242	Calories	5.7 g	Fiber
1.5 g	Fat	658 mg	Sodium
34.9 g	Protein	55 mg	Cholesterol
21.5 g	Carbohydrates		

Diabetic exchanges: Lean meat, 3; starch, 1

Mouthwatering Enchiladas

Serves 2

¾ cup 1 percent cottage cheese
2 green onions, chopped
2 tablespoons seeded and chopped green bell pepper
1 clove garlic, pressed
¼ cup Sargento light grated Cheddar cheese
2 small lowfat flour tortillas
½ cup green chili enchilada sauce
2 tablespoons fat-free sour cream

Preheat oven to 350 degrees F.

In small bowl, combine cottage cheese, green onions, green pepper, and garlic. Add cheese and mix. Softly roll half of the mixture in each tortilla. Place in small baking dish and pour enchilada sauce on top. Bake for 25 minutes. Top with fat-free sour cream before serving.

Each serving provides:

282	Calories	1.6 g	Fiber
5.2 g	Fat	1146 mg	Sodium
18.9 g	Protein	9 mg	Cholesterol
40.6 g	Carbohydrates		

Diabetic exchanges: Lean meat, 2; vegetable, ½; starch, 2

SMOKY SKILLET CHICKEN

SERVES 4

4 boneless, skinless chicken breasts (3 ounces each)
4 slices turkey bacon
   Salt and black pepper
¼ cup Kraft Thick 'n Spicy Honey Barbecue Sauce
3 tablespoons water
½ teaspoon white vinegar

Spray medium skillet with nonstick cooking spray. Wrap each chicken breast with a slice of bacon and place in skillet. Use toothpicks to keep bacon in place until it cooks, then remove.

Season chicken with salt and pepper to taste. In a small bowl, combine honey barbecue sauce, water, and vinegar. Pour mixture over chicken, cover, and simmer over very low heat for about 10 minutes, or until chicken is done.

Each serving provides:

155	Calories	0.2 g	Fiber
3.6 g	Fat	425 mg	Sodium
22.2 g	Protein	59 mg	Cholesterol
6.8 g	Carbohydrates		

Diabetic exchanges: Lean meat, 2½; vegetable, ½

CHICKEN CHILI

SERVES 4

2 boneless, skinless chicken breasts (3 ounces each), cut into very small pieces
2 tablespoons William's chili seasoning
1 can (14½ ounces) stewed tomatoes, chopped, with liquid
2 cloves fresh garlic, pressed
1 small onion, chopped
¼ teaspoon onion powder
1 can (14½ ounces) fat-free chicken broth
1 cup water

Spray medium saucepan with nonstick cooking spray. Place chicken in pan and brown over medium heat. Add chili seasoning, tomatoes, garlic, onion, onion powder, chicken broth, and water. Simmer uncovered over low heat for 45 minutes.

Each serving provides:

107	Calories	1.5 g	Fiber
0.7 g	Fat	771 mg	Sodium
12.3 g	Protein	24 mg	Cholesterol
12.2 g	Carbohydrates		

Diabetic exchanges: Lean meat, 1; vegetable, ½; starch, ½

FIESTA CHICKEN BREASTS WITH CHEESE SAUCE

SERVES 2

1   medium onion, sliced
2   boneless, skinless chicken breasts (3 ounces each)
    Garlic powder
    Onion powder
    Black pepper
1   cup fat-free chicken broth
¼   cup Campbell's condensed Fiesta Nacho cheese soup
2   tablespoons fat-free sour cream
1½ tablespoons cornstarch

Spray medium skillet with nonstick cooking spray. Add onion and brown over medium heat. Season chicken with garlic powder, onion powder, and black pepper to taste. Add chicken to skillet and brown on each side over medium heat. Cover and cook over low heat until done, about 15 minutes.

In a small saucepan, combine chicken broth, cheese soup, sour cream, and cornstarch. Use a whisk to mix and smooth. Cook over medium-low heat until mixture thickens slightly. Serve chicken breast covered with onions and pour cheese sauce over both.

Each serving provides:

193	Calories	1.6 g	Fiber
3.2 g	Fat	763 mg	Sodium
23.7 g	Protein	53 mg	Cholesterol
16 g	Carbohydrates		

Diabetic exchanges: Lean meat, 2; starch, 1

Southwest Chicken Wraps

2 chicken breasts (3 ounces each), cut into thin strips
1 medium to large onion, sliced
1 fresh green chili pepper, seeded and thinly sliced
⅓ cup fat-free mayonnaise
Dash of chili powder
¼ teaspoon garlic powder
Juice of ½ lime
4 fat-free flour tortillas (8 inches each)
1 medium to large avocado, peeled and sliced
1 large tomato, thinly sliced
8 tablespoons Sargento light grated four-cheese Mexican cheese
Garlic salt
Black pepper

Spray medium skillet with nonstick cooking spray. Add chicken, onion, and chili pepper. Cook over low heat until onion and chicken are done, about 15 minutes.

In small bowl, combine mayonnaise, chili powder, garlic powder, and lime juice. Stir and mix thoroughly.

On each tortilla, spread about 1 tablespoon mayonnaise mixture. Place a few chicken pieces, a little cooked onion/pepper mixture, about 2 avocado slices, 2 thin slices of tomato, and 2 tablespoons cheese on each. Add garlic salt and black pepper to taste and roll up.

Each serving provides:

217	Calories	4.7 g	Fiber
10.6 g	Fat	425 mg	Sodium
16.2 g	Protein	29 mg	Cholesterol
16.8 g	Carbohydrates		

Diabetic exchanges: Lean meat, 2; vegetable, 1; starch, 1

Chicken with Roasted Pine Nuts and Cream Sauce

SERVES 2

2	tablespoons chopped pine nuts
2	boneless, skinless chicken breasts (3 ounces each)
1	egg white, slightly beaten
½	cup crushed cornflakes
	Salt and black pepper
1½	tablespoons cornstarch
1	cup fat-free chicken broth
½	teaspoon Molly McButter butter sprinkles
½	teaspoon parsley
	Black pepper
1	tablespoon white cooking wine
3	tablespoons fat-free sour cream

Preheat oven to 350 degrees F.

Spray small pan or skillet with nonstick cooking spray. Add pine nuts and brown lightly over *very* low heat. Set aside to cool.

Dip each chicken breast in egg white. Roll chicken in cornflakes and then in pine nuts. Spray an 8 × 8-inch baking dish with nonstick cooking spray. Place chicken breasts in dish, season with salt and pepper, and bake for 20 to 25 minutes.

Meanwhile, spray small saucepan with nonstick cooking spray. Add cornstarch. Stir in chicken broth gradually over low heat. Add butter sprinkles, parsley, pepper to taste, and white wine. Simmer for 2 to 3 minutes, until sauce starts to thicken. Remove from heat and whisk in fat-free sour cream. Pour sauce over chicken and serve.

Each serving provides:

315	Calories	1.1 g	Fiber
7.3 g	Fat	957 mg	Sodium
28.2 g	Protein	53 mg	Cholesterol
34.7 g	Carbohydrates		

Diabetic exchanges: Lean meat, 2; fat, 1; starch, 2

INDIAN TACO

SERVES 2

2 Pillsbury ready-to-bake biscuits
⅓ pound extra-lean ground beef
1 tablespoon taco seasoning
¼ teaspoon garlic powder
⅓ cup grated fat-free Cheddar or American cheese
1 small onion, chopped
1½ cups shredded lettuce
2 tablespoons fat-free sour cream

Preheat oven to 400 degrees F.

Using a rolling pin, roll out each biscuit to at least double its size. Spray baking sheet or pan with nonstick cooking spray. Place biscuit dough on baking sheet. Bake for 6 to 8 minutes or until golden brown.

MAIN DISHES
190

Spray medium skillet with nonstick cooking spray. Add ground beef and brown over medium heat. Season meat with taco seasoning and garlic powder. Add a few tablespoons of water if needed. Stir and simmer over low heat until meat is cooked thoroughly.

Place each biscuit on a plate. On each biscuit, spoon on half of the meat. Add half the cheese, onion, and lettuce. Top each with 1 tablespoon fat-free sour cream.

Each serving provides:

309	Calories	2 g	Fiber
14.2 g	Fat	808 mg	Sodium
24.1 g	Protein	56 mg	Cholesterol
20.1 g	Carbohydrates		

Diabetic exchanges: Medium meat, 3; starch, 1

Chicken Breasts with Salsa Verde

Serves 4

4 boneless, skinless chicken breasts (3 ounces each)
½ teaspoon garlic powder
½ teaspoon onion powder
Salt and black pepper
½ cup canned salsa verde
1 can (10¾ ounces) 98 percent fat-free condensed cream of mushroom soup
1 small onion, chopped
4 tablespoons fat-free sour cream

Spray medium skillet with nonstick cooking spray. Season both sides of each chicken breast with garlic powder, onion powder, and salt and black pepper to taste. Brown chicken breasts in skillet over medium heat on both sides. Reduce heat to low and simmer for 10 to 12 minutes, until done.

In small saucepan, combine salsa verde, cream of mushroom soup, and onion. Simmer over medium-low heat for 3 to 5 minutes. Whisk sour cream into sauce just before serving. Pour sauce over chicken breasts and serve.

Each serving provides:

145	Calories	0.8 g	Fiber
2.9 g	Fat	274 mg	Sodium
21.2 g	Protein	54 mg	Cholesterol
7.3 g	Carbohydrates		

Diabetic exchanges: Lean meat, 2; vegetable, ½; starch, ⅓

SPINACH AND CHICKEN QUESADILLAS

SERVES 2

1 boneless, skinless chicken breast (4 ounces),
   cut into thin strips
¼ teaspoon garlic powder
   Salt and black pepper
2 fat-free flour tortillas (8 inches in diameter)
6 to 8 small to medium leaves fresh spinach
1 green onion, chopped
3 slices Kraft fat-free American cheese

Spray small skillet with nonstick cooking spray. Brown chicken and season with garlic powder and salt and pepper to taste. Cover and cook slowly over low heat for 10 to 12 minutes, until done. Set aside and let cool.

Spray large skillet with nonstick cooking spray. Place 1 tortilla in skillet and warm over very low heat for 30 to 40 seconds. Turn tortilla over and place spinach leaves evenly over tortilla. Add green onion and cheese. Place chicken on top of cheese and place another tortilla on top. Cover and heat over low heat until cheese melts. Turn tortilla and heat the other side. Slice in half and serve warm.

Each serving provides:

188	Calories	5.9 g	Fiber
1.9 g	Fat	663 mg	Sodium
23.1 g	Protein	35 mg	Cholesterol
19.7 g	Carbohydrates		

Diabetic exchanges: Lean meat, 2; starch, 1

CHEESY CHICKEN

2 boneless, skinless chicken breasts (3 ounces each)
½ teaspoon onion powder
½ plus ⅛ teaspoon garlic powder
   Salt and black pepper
4 tablespoons Old El Paso lowfat cheese and salsa dip
2 tablespoons fat-free sour cream
1 tablespoon Tabasco jalapeño sauce (green)
3 tablespoons skim milk
1 green onion, chopped
   Fresh parsley for garnish (optional)

Spray small skillet with nonstick cooking spray. Season both sides of each chicken breast with onion powder, ½ teaspoon of the garlic powder, and salt and pepper to taste. Brown and cook chicken over low heat for 10 to 12 minutes, until done.

In small saucepan, combine cheese dip, sour cream, jalapeño sauce, skim milk, green onion, and remaining garlic powder. Stir over low heat until warm. Pour sauce over chicken. Garnish with a little parsley if desired.

Each serving provides:

191	Calories	0.3 g	Fiber
4.5 g	Fat	723 mg	Sodium
28.5 g	Protein	70 mg	Cholesterol
7.4 g	Carbohydrates		

Diabetic exchanges: Lean meat, 3; vegetable, 1

3

VEGETABLES AND SIDE DISHES

Jalapeño Corn

SERVES 3

½ cup chopped onion
¼ cup seeded and chopped bell pepper
1 tablespoon fat-free chicken broth or water (if needed)
1 teaspoon minced garlic
1 cup frozen corn, thawed
1 tablespoon vinegar from pickled jalapeños

Spray medium skillet with nonstick cooking spray and lightly sauté onion and bell pepper over medium heat for 5 to 8 minutes. Add chicken broth if extra moisture is needed.

Add garlic, corn, and vinegar. Cover skillet and steam over low to medium heat, stirring occasionally, 8 to 10 minutes.

Each serving provides:

60	Calories	2 g	Fiber
0.3 g	Fat	21 mg	Sodium
2 g	Protein	0 mg	Cholesterol
14.3 g	Carbohydrates		

Diabetic exchange: Starch, ¾

LAYERED VEGGIES

1 teaspoon minced garlic
1 cup diced canned (and drained) or fresh tomatoes
1 tablespoon seeded and chopped serrano peppers
1 cup (8 ounces) tomato sauce
½ teaspoon salt
2 cups sliced squash (crookneck or zucchini,
   or a mixture of both)
1 cup sliced fresh mushrooms
½ cup sliced onion (about ½ onion)
1 cup light Sargento grated Cheddar cheese

Preheat oven to 350 degrees F.

Spray a 9-inch-square baking dish with nonstick cooking spray. Mix garlic, tomatoes, serrano peppers, tomato sauce, and salt together in a small bowl. Layer squash, mushrooms, and onion in baking dish. Pour tomato sauce mixture over all. Top with grated cheese. Cover dish and bake for 30 minutes.

Each serving provides:

128	Calories	3.3 g	Fiber
5 g	Fat	935 mg	Sodium
10.9 g	Protein	10 mg	Cholesterol
13.8 g	Carbohydrates		

Diabetic exchanges: Medium meat, 1; vegetable, ½; starch, ½

Southwest Stuffed Peppers

Serves 3

1 medium onion, chopped
2 slices turkey bacon, cut into small pieces
½ pound ground turkey breast
⅓ cup tomato paste
¼ cup water
½ cup cooked rice
3 to 4 slices seeded jalapeño peppers or green chilies (if you prefer a milder taste)
1 teaspoon Tabasco jalapeño sauce (green)
  Salt and black pepper
3 to 4 large bell peppers, tops cut off and seeded

Preheat oven to 350 degrees F.

Spray medium skillet with nonstick cooking spray. Add onion, bacon, and ground turkey and brown over medium heat. Add tomato paste and water and stir. Add rice, jalapeño peppers or green chilies, jalapeño sauce, salt and pepper to taste. Remove from heat and stir.

    Stuff meat mixture into bell peppers and place in small baking dish. Bake for 35 to 45 minutes.

Each serving provides:

218	Calories	3.7 g	Fiber
3.5 g	Fat	485 mg	Sodium
22.9 g	Protein	52 mg	Cholesterol
24.5 g	Carbohydrates		

Diabetic exchanges: Lean meat, 2; starch, 1¼

Macaroni Casserole

1   tablespoon chopped canned green chilies
1   small onion, chopped
¼   cup seeded and chopped green bell pepper
1   cup cooked macaroni
1½ teaspoons Molly McButter butter sprinkles
¼   cup evaporated skim milk
2   tablespoons fat-free sour cream
    Dash of dried oregano
    Dash of garlic powder
    Dash of onion powder
    Salt and black pepper
½   cup Sargento light grated Cheddar cheese

Preheat oven to 350 degrees F.

In medium bowl, combine chilies, onion, bell pepper, macaroni, butter sprinkles, skim milk, sour cream, oregano, garlic
powder, onion powder, salt and pepper to taste, and ¼ cup
of cheese. Mix well. Spray glass loaf pan with nonstick cooking spray. Pour in mixture and top with remaining cheese.
Bake for 30 to 35 minutes.

Each serving provides:

231	Calories	2.3 g	Fiber
5.2 g	Fat	388 mg	Sodium
15.5 g	Protein	11 mg	Cholesterol
31.7 g	Carbohydrates		

Diabetic exchanges: Lean meat, 2; starch, 1½

Fiesta Potato Salad

Serves 4

¼   cup fat-free mayonnaise
¼   cup (4 ounces) Kraft fat-free cream cheese
¼   teaspoon prepared spicy mustard
¼   teaspoon horseradish
½   clove garlic, pressed
⅛   teaspoon black pepper
2   medium red potatoes, cooked and cubed
1   small onion, chopped
2½ tablespoons seeded and chopped green bell pepper
2½ tablespoons grated carrot
2½ tablespoons chopped celery
6   tablespoons crushed oil-free tortilla chips

In medium bowl, combine mayonnaise, cream cheese, mustard, horseradish, garlic, and pepper. Mix.

In large bowl, combine potatoes, onion, green pepper, carrot, and celery. Add dressing to salad and toss. Refrigerate 2 to 3 hours. Just before serving, sprinkle 1½ tablespoons tortilla chips over each serving.

Each serving provides:

152	Calories	4 g	Fiber
0.5 g	Fat	338 mg	Sodium
6.4 g	Protein	5 mg	Cholesterol
30.3 g	Carbohydrates		

Diabetic exchanges: Lean meat, ½; vegetable, 1; starch, 1¼

SWEET-HOT CARROTS

SERVES 3

1 cup sliced fresh carrots
⅓ cup pineapple juice (see below)
1 teaspoon Brown Sugar Twin sweetener
1 teaspoon Molly McButter butter sprinkles
2 teaspoons cornstarch
½ cup pineapple tidbits, reserve juice
½ teaspoon red pepper flakes
3 tablespoons Equal sweetener

Steam or cook carrots in saucepan over medium-low heat for 15 to 20 minutes, until done.

In small saucepan, combine pineapple juice, brown sugar sweetener, butter sprinkles, and cornstarch. Stir over medium-low heat until sauce starts to thicken. Remove sauce from heat. Add pineapple, red pepper flakes, and sweetener and stir. Pour over warm carrots.

Each serving provides:

76	Calories	1.2 g	Fiber
0.1 g	Fat	95 mg	Sodium
2.1 g	Protein	0 mg	Cholesterol
17 g	Carbohydrates		

Diabetic exchanges: Vegetable, 2; fruit, ½

Southwest Baked Beans with Jalapeño

Serves 4

1   can (15 ounces) lowfat pork and beans
½   small jalapeño pepper, seeded and chopped
2   teaspoons Brown Sugar Twin sweetener
½   small onion, chopped
2   tablespoons ketchup
⅛   teaspoon dry mustard
2   slices maple-smoked turkey bacon, cut into pieces
   Salt and black pepper

Preheat oven to 375 degrees F.

In medium bowl, combine pork and beans, jalapeño pepper, brown sugar sweetener, onion, ketchup, mustard, bacon, and salt and pepper to taste. Spray glass loaf pan with non-stick cooking spray. Add mixture to pan. Bake for 35 to 45 minutes.

Each serving provides:

154	Calories	7.3 g	Fiber
2.6 g	Fat	741 mg	Sodium
8.1 g	Protein	14 mg	Cholesterol
28.1 g	Carbohydrates		

Diabetic exchanges: Vegetable, 1½; starch, 1½

Smothered Red Onions

Serves 3

1 extra-large red onion, cut into medium-thick slices
1 slice turkey bacon, cut into small pieces
1 clove garlic, pressed
  Salt and black pepper

Spray medium skillet with nonstick cooking spray. Add onion, bacon, and garlic. Simmer and brown over medium-low heat, stirring occasionally, until onions are soft and light brown in color. Season with salt and pepper.

These are a wonderful complement to any meal. Serve over meat, vegetables, and potatoes or as a side dish.

Each serving provides:

37	Calories	1.2 g	Fiber
1 g	Fat	63 mg	Sodium
1.6 g	Protein	3 mg	Cholesterol
5.9 g	Carbohydrates		

Diabetic exchanges: Lean meat, ⅕; vegetable, 1

Mexican Cheese Biscuits

¾ cup Pioneer lowfat biscuit mix
⅓ cup skim milk
1 green onion, chopped
¼ to ½ small fresh green chili pepper, seeded
  and chopped
¼ cup Sargento light grated Cheddar cheese

Preheat oven to 400 degrees F.

In medium bowl, combine all ingredients and mix well. Spray baking sheet or pan with nonstick cooking spray. Drop dough by spoonfuls onto baking sheet. Bake for 12 to 14 minutes.

Each serving provides:

279	Calories	1.3 g	Fiber
3.1 g	Fat	888 mg	Sodium
10.1 g	Protein	6 mg	Cholesterol
63.5 g	Carbohydrates		

Diabetic exchanges: Lean meat, 1; vegetable, 1; starch, 2½

Garlic Mashed Potatoes with Jalapeño

1 large potato, peeled and cut into chunks
2 cloves of garlic, peeled
3 tablespoons white cooking wine
2 tablespoons Molly McButter butter sprinkles
1 to 2 tablespoons evaporated skim milk
½ fresh jalapeño pepper, seeded and finely chopped

Place potato in medium saucepan and cover with water. Cook over medium-low heat until tender, 20 to 25 minutes.

While potatoes are cooking, place garlic, wine, and 1 tablespoon butter sprinkles in small saucepan. Cover and cook over very low heat for about 20 minutes or until garlic is tender. Mash garlic with fork.

Drain water from potatoes. Add milk and remaining butter sprinkles and mash using an electric mixer. Add garlic mixture to potatoes while mashing, and then add jalapeño pepper and mix well.

Each serving provides:

71	Calories	2.4 g	Fiber
0.1 g	Fat	405 mg	Sodium
1.7 g	Protein	0 mg	Cholesterol
15 g	Carbohydrates		

Diabetic exchange: Starch, 1

Mexican Macaroni and Cheese

⅓   cup fat-free chicken broth
1   tablespoon very finely chopped onion
¼   cup Old El Paso lowfat cheese and salsa dip
2   tablespoons fat-free sour cream
¼   teaspoon taco seasoning
1   small clove garlic, pressed
    Salt and black pepper
1½ cups cooked macaroni or your favorite pasta

In small saucepan, combine chicken broth and onion, then simmer over low heat for 4 to 5 minutes, until onion is cooked. Add cheese dip, sour cream, taco seasoning, garlic, and salt and pepper to taste and whisk until smooth. Continue to stir over low heat for about 2 minutes—do not boil. Pour this mixture over macaroni and serve.

Each serving provides:

195	Calories	1.8 g	Fiber
2.2 g	Fat	479 mg	Sodium
7.4 g	Protein	0 mg	Cholesterol
35.7 g	Carbohydrates		

Diabetic exchanges: Lean meat, 1½; starch, 1½

Jalapeño Corn Fritters

¼ cup all-purpose flour
⅓ cup cornmeal
½ teaspoon salt
½ teaspoon baking powder
½ teaspoon Molly McButter butter sprinkles
2 tablespoons Equal sweetener
¼ cup skim milk
¼ cup fat-free liquid egg product
½ fresh jalapeño pepper, seeded and finely chopped

Spray large skillet with nonstick cooking spray. In medium bowl, combine flour, cornmeal, salt, baking powder, butter sprinkles, and sweetener and mix well. Add milk, egg product, and jalapeño pepper and mix well. Spoon batter into skillet in small portions (about 1 tablespoon). Brown on one side over medium-high heat and turn to brown on the other.

Each serving provides:

61	Calories	0.6 g	Fiber
0.2 g	Fat	256 mg	Sodium
3.1 g	Protein	0 mg	Cholesterol
11.4 g	Carbohydrates		

Diabetic exchanges: Milk, ⅕; starch, ½

Tex-Mex Rice with Hot and Spicy Flair

Serves 4

2   cups rice
2   teaspoons Molly McButter butter sprinkles
½   small onion, chopped
1½   tablespoons chopped canned green chilies
2   tablespoons Tabasco jalapeño sauce (green)
¼   cup fat-free chicken broth
     Dash of chili powder
     Salt and black pepper

Cook rice according to package directions (add butter sprinkles to rice toward the end of cooking).

Spray large skillet with nonstick cooking spray. Add onion and cook over medium-high heat until onion is browned. Add rice, chilies, jalapeño sauce, chicken broth, chili powder, and salt and pepper to taste. Simmer over low heat, stirring occasionally, until all liquid is gone. Serve by itself or with any Mexican meal.

Each serving provides:

352	Calories	1.3 g	Fiber
0.7 g	Fat	521 mg	Sodium
7 g	Protein	0 mg	Cholesterol
76.9 g	Carbohydrates		

Diabetic exchange: Starch, 4½

CHEESE FRIES, TEX-MEX STYLE

1 large potato
  Seasoned salt
  Black pepper
2 tablespoons Tostitos salsa con queso (cheese dip)

Preheat oven to 375 degrees F.

Peel potato and cut like French fries. Spray baking sheet with butter-flavored nonstick cooking spray. Arrange potato slices on baking sheet, preferably not touching. Spray the potatoes lightly with nonstick cooking spray and sprinkle with seasoned salt and pepper to taste. Bake for 35 to 40 minutes or until potatoes are light brown.

Warm cheese dip in microwave until it pours easily (about 30 seconds on high). Drizzle cheese over fries and serve.

Each serving provides:

73	Calories	1.3 g	Fiber
1.1 g	Fat	329 mg	Sodium
1.9 g	Protein	2 mg	Cholesterol
14.6 g	Carbohydrates		

Diabetic exchange: Starch, 1

Skillet Southwest Potatoes

Serves 3

2 slices turkey bacon
1 medium potato, peeled and cut into small chunks
½ small onion, diced
1 teaspoon Molly McButter butter sprinkles
Salt and black pepper

Spray large skillet with nonstick cooking spray. Use kitchen scissors and cut bacon into bite-size pieces. Put bacon pieces into skillet. Add potato, onion, butter sprinkles, and salt and pepper to taste. Cook and stir over medium heat until potatoes are golden brown.

Each serving provides:

52	Calories	0.6 g	Fiber
1.7 g	Fat	189 mg	Sodium
2.4 g	Protein	7 mg	Cholesterol
7.2 g	Carbohydrates		

Diabetic exchange: Starch, ¾

TACO CORN

8 ounces frozen corn, thawed
1 fresh green chili, seeded and chopped
½ tablespoon Molly McButter butter sprinkles
½ teaspoon taco seasoning
1 teaspoon dry onion flakes
¼ cup water

In saucepan, combine all ingredients. Simmer over low heat until corn is done and most of the water has cooked away.

Each serving provides:

53	Calories	1.6 g	Fiber
0.3 g	Fat	98 mg	Sodium
1.8 g	Protein	0 mg	Cholesterol
12.9 g	Carbohydrates		

Diabetic exchanges: Vegetable, ½; starch, ½

POSOLE CASSEROLE

1   can (16 ounces) hominy
½   small onion, chopped
1   tablespoon chopped pimientos
1   can (10¾ ounces) Campbell's 98 percent fat-free
    condensed cream of mushroom soup
⅓   cup canned sliced mushrooms, drained
¼   cup fat-free chicken broth
¼   cup fat-free sour cream
1½ teaspoons Molly McButter butter sprinkles
¼   cup Sargento light grated Cheddar cheese
    Salt and black pepper
¼   cup crushed cornflakes

Preheat oven to 350 degrees F.

In medium bowl, combine hominy, onion, pimientos, cream
of mushroom soup, mushrooms, chicken broth, sour cream,
butter sprinkles, cheese, and salt and pepper to taste and

mix thoroughly. Pour into small casserole sprayed with nonstick cooking spray. Top with cornflakes. Bake for 35 to 45 minutes.

Each serving provides:

161	Calories	2.1 g	Fiber
1.9 g	Fat	854 mg	Sodium
6.1 g	Protein	4 mg	Cholesterol
30 g	Carbohydrates		

Diabetic exchange: Starch, 2

Southwest Potato Salad

1 large potato, boiled, peeled, and chopped
2 green onions, chopped
2 hard-boiled eggs, peeled and yolks discarded
   (use egg whites only), chopped
1 tablespoon chopped dill pickle
1 tablespoon chopped sweet pickle
1 tablespoon seeded and chopped bell pepper
½ fresh mild green chili pepper, seeded and chopped
¼ cup finely grated carrot
   Salt and black pepper
⅓ cup fat-free mayonnaise
1 teaspoon prepared mustard
   Juice of ½ lime
1 clove garlic, pressed
1 tablespoon fat-free sour cream

In medium bowl, combine potato, green onions, eggs, dill and sweet pickle, bell pepper, chili pepper, carrot, and salt and pepper to taste. Mix.

In small bowl, combine mayonnaise, mustard, lime juice, garlic, and sour cream and mix. Add dressing to potato salad and mix well. Chill slightly before serving.

Each serving provides:

105	Calories	3.1 g	Fiber
0.2 g	Fat	523 mg	Sodium
4.3 g	Protein	0 mg	Cholesterol
22.2 g	Carbohydrates		

Diabetic exchanges: Vegetable, 1; starch, 1

Baked Artichokes with Green Chilies

Serves 3

½   cup fat-free liquid egg product
¼   cup evaporated skim milk
1   teaspoon Molly McButter butter sprinkles
1   tablespoon all-purpose flour
2½ tablespoons fat-free sour cream
1   can (14 ounces) artichoke hearts, drained,
    cut into quarters
2   tablespoons chopped canned green chilies
1   teaspoon dry onion flakes
¼   cup Sargento light grated Cheddar cheese
    Salt and black pepper

Preheat oven to 350 degrees F.

In large bowl, combine egg product, milk, and butter sprinkles and mix using electric mixer. Continue mixing and gradually add flour, then sour cream. Stir in artichoke hearts, chilies, onion flakes, and cheese with a spoon. Add salt and black pepper to taste.

Pour mixture into 9-inch casserole pan sprayed with nonstick cooking spray and bake for 45 minutes.

Each serving provides:

112	Calories	1.2 g	Fiber
1.7 g	Fat	467 mg	Sodium
11.4 g	Protein	4 mg	Cholesterol
13.8 g	Carbohydrates		

Diabetic exchanges: Lean meat, 1; vegetable, 2

Onion Layered Corn Bread

Serves 6

1½ large sweet onions, sliced
½   teaspoon garlic salt
⅛   teaspoon black pepper
½   cup Kraft fat-free cream cheese
1¼ cups lowfat buttermilk
1   tablespoon sugar
¼   teaspoon salt
1   egg white
1¼ cups cornmeal
½   teaspoon baking soda
2   teaspoons baking powder
½   cup Sargento light grated Cheddar cheese

Preheat oven to 400 degrees F.

Spray large skillet with nonstick cooking spray. Add onions and brown over medium heat. Season with garlic salt while browning. Cook onions over low heat until slightly limp. Remove from heat and add pepper and cream cheese; set aside.

In large bowl, combine buttermilk, sugar, salt, and egg white and mix using electric mixer. In another bowl, combine cornmeal, baking soda, and baking powder. Mix thoroughly. Add to buttermilk mixture and mix with electric mixer. Fold in cheese.

Spray medium casserole with nonstick cooking spray. Spread half the onion mixture in casserole. Pour half the batter over onions. Repeat layers. Bake for 30 to 35 minutes.

Each serving provides:

184	Calories	1.8 g	Fiber
2.4 g	Fat	585 mg	Sodium
10.3 g	Protein	8 mg	Cholesterol
30.5 g	Carbohydrates		

Diabetic exchanges: Lean meat, 2; starch, 1

Tex-Mex
Beans and Rice

½ small onion, chopped
1 cup canned brown beans, drained
2½ tablespoons chopped green chilies
6 tablespoons green chili enchilada sauce
2 teaspoons taco seasoning
⅛ teaspoon garlic powder
⅛ teaspoon black pepper
2½ tablespoons water
Seasoned salt
Crushed red pepper (optional)
1 cup cooked rice
¼ cup Sargento light grated Cheddar cheese

Spray medium skillet with nonstick cooking spray. Add onion and brown over medium heat. Add brown beans, chilies, enchilada sauce, taco seasoning, garlic powder, black pepper, water, seasoned salt to taste, and crushed red pepper if desired. Simmer over very low heat for 15 minutes. Serve over rice and top with grated cheese.

Each serving provides:

359	Calories	10.7 g	Fiber
4.6 g	Fat	1199 mg	Sodium
16.5 g	Protein	5 mg	Cholesterol
65.7 g	Carbohydrates		

Diabetic exchanges: Lean meat, 1½; starch, 3½

STUFFED CORNBREAD

SERVES 4

½   pound ground turkey breast or chicken breast
2½ tablespoons water
2   teaspoons taco seasoning
1¼ cups yellow cornmeal
1   tablespoon sugar
¼   teaspoon salt
½   teaspoon baking soda
½   teaspoon baking powder
2   to 3 packets Sweet 'n Low sweetener
1   egg white, slightly beaten
1¼ cups lowfat buttermilk
1   medium onion, chopped
½   cup Sargento light grated Cheddar cheese

Preheat oven to 400 degrees F.

Spray medium skillet with nonstick cooking spray. Add ground turkey or chicken and brown over medium heat. Add water and taco seasoning and simmer over low heat until all liquid is absorbed. Set aside.

In large mixing bowl, combine cornmeal, sugar, salt, baking soda, baking powder, and sweetener and mix well. In small bowl, combine egg white with buttermilk and mix. Add buttermilk mixture to dry ingredients and stir. Stir only long enough to mix ingredients well, but batter should remain slightly lumpy.

Spray an 8-inch-square baking pan or glass baking dish with nonstick cooking spray. Pour half of cornbread batter evenly over bottom. Add all the meat, sprinkled evenly, for the next layer. Add onion as the next layer and then cheese. Pour the remaining cornbread batter evenly over the top. Bake for 30 to 35 minutes.

Each serving provides:

348	Calories	3.3 g	Fiber
8.5 g	Fat	939 mg	Sodium
21.7 g	Protein	53 mg	Cholesterol
45.8 g	Carbohydrates		

Diabetic exchanges: Lean meat, 2; starch, 3

Sweet-Hot Marinated Carrot Rounds

3 large carrots, peeled and sliced
2 tablespoons white vinegar
½ cup water
¼ cup Equal sweetener
   Jalapeño pepper slices, to taste
1 teaspoon dry onion flakes
1 clove garlic, whole

Combine all ingredients in medium bowl and mix. Chill and serve. I like to keep these in the refrigerator for a healthy snack.

Each serving provides:

44	Calories	2.4 g	Fiber
0.1 g	Fat	28 mg	Sodium
2.9 g	Protein	0 mg	Cholesterol
8.8 g	Carbohydrates		

Diabetic exchange: Vegetable, 1¾

Ranch Skillet Potatoes

2 medium potatoes, peeled and cubed
2½ tablespoons chopped onion
½ ounce dry ranch dressing mix
¼ cup fat-free sour cream
1 cup skim milk
¼ teaspoon chopped parsley

Cook potatoes in microwave on high for 2 to 4 minutes, until slightly tender. Spray large skillet with nonstick cooking spray. Brown onion and potatoes over medium-high heat. Cook until potatoes are golden brown. Add dressing mix, sour cream, milk, and parsley and simmer over low heat until sauce thickens. Serve warm. This is a great side dish with almost any meal.

Each serving provides:

100	Calories	1.5 g	Fiber
0.2 g	Fat	736 mg	Sodium
5.3 g	Protein	1 mg	Cholesterol
19.5 g	Carbohydrates		

Diabetic exchanges: Vegetable, 1; starch, 1

SOUTHWEST CORN FRITTERS

⅓ cup all-purpose flour
¾ teaspoon sugar
½ teaspoon salt
1 teaspoon baking powder
1 cup canned corn, drained
2½ tablespoons chopped canned green chilies
1 egg white, slightly beaten
¼ cup skim milk

In medium bowl, combine flour, sugar, salt, and baking powder and stir thoroughly. Add corn, chilies, egg white, and milk and mix. Spray medium skillet with butter-flavored nonstick cooking spray and warm over medium heat. Drop medium-sized spoonfuls of batter into skillet. Brown on one side, then turn and brown on the other side. Repeat for remaining batter.

Each serving provides:

59	Calories	0.7 g	Fiber
0.4 g	Fat	344 mg	Sodium
2.5 g	Protein	0 mg	Cholesterol
12.3 g	Carbohydrates		

Diabetic exchange: Starch, ¾

Mexican Skillet Potatoes

1 small onion, chopped
1 medium potato, peeled and cut into small chunks
2 tablespoons chopped canned green chilies
   Garlic salt
   Black pepper

Spray large skillet with nonstick cooking spray. Add onion, potato and chilies. Cook and brown over low heat until potatoes are done, 15 to 20 minutes. Add garlic salt and black pepper to taste.

Each serving provides:

76	Calories	2.2 g	Fiber
0.2 g	Fat	13 mg	Sodium
1.7 g	Protein	0 mg	Cholesterol
17.5 g	Carbohydrates		

Diabetic exchange: Starch, 1

Jalapeño Corn Bread with Cheese

Serves 6

1¼ cups yellow cornmeal
1 tablespoon sugar
3 packets Sweet 'n Low sweetener
¼ teaspoon salt
¼ teaspoon baking soda
½ tablespoon baking powder
1 egg white, slightly beaten
1¼ cups lowfat buttermilk
⅛ cup seeded and chopped jalapeño peppers (see note)
½ cup Sargento light grated Cheddar cheese

Note: You may substitute peppers with green chilies if you prefer a milder taste.

Preheat oven to 400 degrees F.

In large bowl, mix cornmeal, sugar, sweetener, salt, baking soda, and baking powder. Stir until mixed well and set aside. In small bowl, combine egg white and buttermilk. Add this mixture to dry ingredients and mix. Add jalapeño peppers and stir.

Spray a 9-inch-square pan with nonstick cooking spray. Pour in half the batter. Sprinkle cheese evenly over entire surface of batter. Pour remaining batter on top of cheese layer. Bake for 30 to 35 minutes.

Each serving provides:

164	Calories	1.6 g	Fiber
2.4 g	Fat	315 mg	Sodium
7.5 g	Protein	5 mg	Cholesterol
28.3 g	Carbohydrates		

Diabetic exchanges: Lean meat, 1; skim milk, ⅓; starch, 1

Mexican Corn Bread

¼ cup all-purpose flour
¾ cup cornmeal
2 packets Sweet 'n Low sweetener
1½ teaspoons baking powder
¼ teaspoon salt
¼ cup fat-free liquid egg product
1 teaspoon olive oil
½ cup skim milk
½ cup frozen corn, thawed
2 green onions, chopped
2 teaspoons seeded and chopped green chilies or jalapeños (if you prefer hotter)
½ teaspoon Molly McButter butter sprinkles

Preheat oven to 400 degrees F.

In medium bowl, combine flour, cornmeal, sweetener, baking powder, and salt and mix. Add egg product, olive oil, milk, corn, green onions, chilies, and butter sprinkles and stir.

Spray an 8-inch-square baking dish with nonstick cooking spray. Pour in batter and bake for 15 to 18 minutes.

Each serving provides:

175	Calories	2.3 g	Fiber
1.8 g	Fat	405 mg	Sodium
6.3 g	Protein	1 mg	Cholesterol
33.8 g	Carbohydrates		

Diabetic exchanges: Lean meat, 1; starch, 1½

Stuffed Anaheim Peppers

¾ cup 1 percent cottage cheese
1 green onion, chopped
1 clove garlic, pressed
2 tablespoons Sargento light grated Cheddar cheese
  Dash of chili powder
2 tablespoons fat-free liquid egg product
2 fresh Anaheim peppers (7 to 8 inches long), sliced open
  lengthwise and seeded

Preheat oven to 350 degrees F.

In small bowl, combine cottage cheese, green onion, garlic, cheese, chili powder, and egg product.

Fill center of each pepper with cottage cheese mixture. Place peppers in glass loaf pan side by side.

Bake for 40 minutes.

Each serving provides:

127	Calories	1.8 g	Fiber
2.2 g	Fat	428 mg	Sodium
16 g	Protein	6 mg	Cholesterol
12.3 g	Carbohydrates		

Diabetic exchanges: Lean meat, 1½; vegetable, 2

Southwest Potato Casserole

2 cups shredded frozen hash brown potatoes, thawed
3 tablespoons fat-free liquid egg product
½ teaspoon garlic powder
2 tablespoons chopped canned green chilies
2 tablespoons fat-free sour cream
  Salt and black pepper

Preheat oven to 400 degrees F.

In small bowl, combine potatoes, egg product, garlic powder, chilies, sour cream, and salt and pepper to taste. Mix thoroughly. Spray a loaf pan or baking dish with nonstick cooking spray. Spread potato mixture in pan and bake for 20 to 25 minutes.

Each serving provides:

66	Calories	1.4 g	Fiber
0.3 g	Fat	48 mg	Sodium
3.1 g	Protein	0 mg	Cholesterol
12.8 g	Carbohydrates		

Diabetic exchanges: Lean meat, ½; starch, ½

4

DESSERTS AND SWEET THINGS

ALICE'S VERY SPECIAL CHOCOLATE PUDDING

SERVES 6

1 package (1.2 ounces) Jell-O cook-and-serve chocolate pudding mix
2 cups skim milk
¼ cup fat-free liquid egg product
2 tablespoons semisweet chocolate chips, melted
1 teaspoon vanilla

Prepare pudding according to directions on package using skim milk. When pudding begins to thicken in saucepan, stir in egg product and melted chocolate. Stir constantly for about 2 minutes. Remove from heat and add vanilla, stirring well.

Each serving provides:

163	Calories	0.1 g	Fiber
2.4 g	Fat	255 mg	Sodium
6 g	Protein	2 mg	Cholesterol
30 g	Carbohydrates		

Diabetic exchanges: Skim milk, ½; starch, 1½

CREAMY FRUIT REFRIGERATOR DESSERT

SERVES 6

½ cup lowfat cinnamon graham cracker crumbs
1 teaspoon Brown Sugar Twin sweetener
1 tub (8 ounces) soft fat-free cream cheese
1 teaspoon vanilla
½ cup fat-free vanilla yogurt
3 packets Sweet 'n Low sweetener
¼ cup peach slices
¼ cup apricot slices
¼ cup pineapple pieces
¼ cup banana slices

Mix together graham cracker crumbs and brown sugar sweetener. Sprinkle evenly over 9-inch pie plate or square pan sprayed with Buttermist or other butter-flavored non-stick cooking spray.

Using an electric mixer in medium mixing bowl, beat together cream cheese, vanilla, yogurt, and sweetener until smooth. Carefully pour and spread mixture over crumbs.

Combine fruit in separate bowl, stirring gently. Spoon fruit over cream cheese mixture. Cover and refrigerate at least 1½ hours until ready to serve.

Each serving provides:

104	Calories	0.9 g	Fiber
0.1 g	Fat	227 mg	Sodium
7.6 g	Protein	3 mg	Cholesterol
17.8 g	Carbohydrates		

Diabetic exchanges: Skim milk, ½; fruit, 1

Hot Cinnamon Fruit Sauce

Serves 6

½ cup peach slices
½ cup pineapple pieces
½ cup apricot slices
½ cup pear slices
⅓ cup liquid Butter Buds
1 tablespoon pineapple juice
1 tablespoon Brown Sugar Twin sweetener
½ teaspoon cinnamon
⅛ teaspoon pumpkin pie spice

If using canned fruits, choose those packed in juice. Save pineapple juice for use in recipe. Stir all ingredients together in saucepan; heat over medium heat to boiling. Remove from heat.

Serve over sugar-free ice cream.

Each serving provides:

35	Calories	1.3 g	Fiber
0.2 g	Fat	83 mg	Sodium
0.4 g	Protein	0 mg	Cholesterol
8.8 g	Carbohydrates		

Diabetic exchange: Fruit, ½

CREAMY FRUIT DESSERT

SERVES 2

½ cup fresh strawberry slices
1 banana, sliced
½ cup fresh or frozen blueberries (if using frozen, thawed)
½ cup pineapple chunks or tidbits
  Juice of ½ small lemon
½ cup fat-free sour cream
3 tablespoons Equal sweetener
¼ teaspoon vanilla

In medium bowl, combine strawberries, banana, blueberries, and pineapple and stir. Squeeze lemon juice over fruit. In small bowl, combine sour cream, sweetener, and vanilla and mix.

Divide fruit into 2 bowls or servings. Top with sauce and serve.

Each serving provides:

168	Calories	3.8 g	Fiber
0.6 g	Fat	44 mg	Sodium
7.5 g	Protein	0 mg	Cholesterol
35.5 g	Carbohydrates		

Diabetic exchanges: Skim milk, ½; fruit, 2

PISTACHIO CREAM DESSERT

SERVES 4

Crust

¼ cup lowfat graham cracker crumbs
1 tablespoon Equal sweetener
¼ teaspoon Molly McButter butter sprinkles

Filling

1 tub (8 ounces) fat-free cream cheese
⅓ cup Equal sweetener
1 teaspoon vanilla
1 package (1 ounce) sugar-free pistachio instant pudding
2 cups skim milk

To make crust, in small bowl, mix graham cracker crumbs, sweetener, and butter sprinkles.

Spray glass loaf pan with nonstick cooking spray. Sprinkle graham cracker mixture onto bottom of loaf pan. Set aside.

To make filling, in medium bowl, combine cream cheese, sweetener, and vanilla. Beat using a mixer until smooth.

In another bowl, mix instant pudding according to package directions using skim milk. Add cream cheese mixture and continue to mix, approximately 1 minute. Pour into glass loaf pan and chill for several hours before serving.

Each serving provides:

164	Calories	0.3 g	Fiber
0.2 g	Fat	688 mg	Sodium
15.6 g	Protein	6 mg	Cholesterol
22 g	Carbohydrates		

Diabetic exchanges: Lean meat, ¾; skim milk, ½; starch, 1

Cinnamon Apple Rolls

Serves 4

1 cup canned apple slices (no sugar added), cut into small pieces

⅓ cup Equal sweetener

1 teaspoon cinnamon

2 teaspoons Molly McButter butter sprinkles

4 egg roll wrappers

1 egg white, slightly beaten

Preheat oven to 375 degrees F.

In small bowl, combine apple, sweetener, cinnamon, and butter sprinkles. Stir until well mixed. Set aside.

Spray baking sheet or pan with nonstick cooking spray. One at a time, dip egg roll wrappers in egg white. Place on plate and spoon about ¼ cup apple mixture onto egg roll wrapper. Roll and wrap like a package and place on baking sheet. Repeat for remaining wrappers. Bake for 25 to 30 minutes.

Each serving provides:

142	Calories	1.7 g	Fiber
0.2 g	Fat	158 mg	Sodium
7 g	Protein	0 mg	Cholesterol
29 g	Carbohydrates		

Diabetic exchanges: Fruit, 1; starch, 1

Chocolate Pancakes

Serves 3 (2 pancakes per serving)

½ cup all-purpose flour
½ teaspoon salt
½ teaspoon baking powder
½ teaspoon Molly McButter butter sprinkles
1 tablespoon Hershey's unsweetened cocoa powder
1 tablespoon mini chocolate chips
¼ cup Equal sweetener
½ cup skim milk
3 tablespoons fat-free liquid egg product

In medium bowl, combine flour, salt, baking powder, butter sprinkles, and cocoa powder and mix well. Add chocolate chips, sweetener, milk, and egg product and mix.

Spray skillet with nonstick cooking spray. Heat skillet over medium heat. Spoon about 2 heaping tablespoons of batter into skillet. Cook on one side over medium-low heat until brown and then turn. Repeat for remaining batter.

Each serving provides:

141	Calories	0.7 g	Fiber
2.3 g	Fat	524 mg	Sodium
7.7 g	Protein	1 mg	Cholesterol
22.7 g	Carbohydrates		

Diabetic exchanges: Lean meat, 1; skim milk, $\frac{1}{10}$; starch, 1

Apple-Cinnamon Pancakes

Serves 3 (2 pancakes per serving)

½ cup all-purpose flour
½ teaspoon salt
½ teaspoon baking powder
⅓ cup skim milk
3 tablespoons fat-free liquid egg product
1 teaspoon cinnamon
⅓ cup chopped fresh apple
3 tablespoons Equal sweetener
½ teaspoon Molly McButter butter sprinkles
¼ teaspoon vanilla

In medium bowl, combine flour, salt, and baking powder and mix well. Add milk, egg product, cinnamon, apple, sweetener, butter sprinkles, and vanilla and mix.

Spray skillet with nonstick cooking spray. Heat skillet over medium heat. Spoon about 2 heaping tablespoons of batter into skillet. Turn when top side starts to bubble and underside is brown. Repeat for remaining batter.

Each serving provides:

131	Calories	1.9 g	Fiber
0.4 g	Fat	515 mg	Sodium
6.2 g	Protein	0 mg	Cholesterol
25.7 g	Carbohydrates		

Diabetic exchanges: Lean meat, ½; fruit, ½; starch, 1

INDEX

INTERNATIONAL CONVERSION CHART

These are not exact equivalents: they've been slightly rounded to make measuring easier.

LIQUID MEASUREMENTS

American	Imperial	Metric	Australian
2 tablespoons (1 oz.)	1 fl. oz.	30 ml	1 tablespoon
¼ cup (2 oz.)	2 fl. oz.	60 ml	2 tablespoons
⅓ cup (3 oz.)	3 fl. oz.	80 ml	¼ cup
½ cup (4 oz.)	4 fl. oz.	125 ml	⅓ cup
⅔ cup (5 oz.)	5 fl. oz.	165 ml	½ cup
¾ cup (6 oz.)	6 fl. oz.	185 ml	⅔ cup
1 cup (8 oz.)	8 fl. oz.	250 ml	¾ cup

SPOON MEASUREMENTS

American	Metric
¼ teaspoon	1 ml
½ teaspoon	2 ml
1 teaspoon	5 ml
1 tablepoon	15 ml

OVEN TEMPERATURES

Fahrenheit	Centigrade	Gas
250	120	½
300	150	2
325	160	3
350	180	4
375	190	5
400	200	6
450	230	8

WEIGHTS

US/UK	Metric
1 oz.	30 grams (g)
2 oz.	60 g
4 oz. (¼ lb)	125 g
5 oz. (⅓ lb)	155 g
6 oz.	185 g
7 oz.	220 g
8 oz. (½ lb)	250 g
10 oz.	315 g
12 oz. (¾ lb)	375 g
14 oz.	440 g
16 oz. (1 lb)	500 g
2 lbs.	1 kg

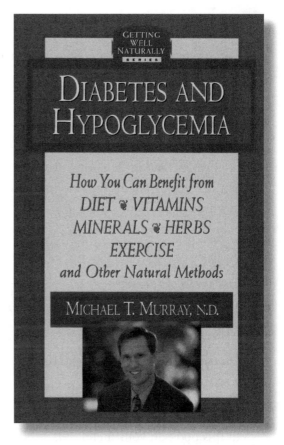

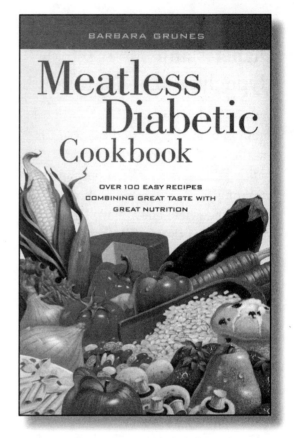